The Art Collector of Le Marais

By Ahmad Ardalan

Copyright 2019 Ahmad Ardalan

"A picture is a poem without words"

Horace

Table of Contents

Prologue

"One hundred and fifty million pounds for Signor Arthur once again," says the old Italian from Lecce.

Sighs erupt all over the room.

"One hundred and fifty million?" a quirky, low voice resonates from among the throng in attendance.

"Shh!"

"One hundred and fifty million pounds, going once...going twice...going—"

"One hundred and seventy!" cries the distinctive voice of Mr. Arnold from the third row. The private dealer is tall and fair-skinned, with pencil-line mustache on his face, dressed in a distinguished gray and black pin-striped suit.

The sighs and gasps echo even louder throughout the eighteenth-century auction house in Central London on the beautiful Monday, May 17, 2010. It has been a brutal cat-and-mouse game between the two gentlemen for at least twenty minutes; the early contenders ceased their bids as soon as the painting price rocketed above thirty-five million pounds.

Arthur nods respectfully to Arnold, conceding in silence, then stands and makes his way out of the room.

"One hundred and seventy million pounds going once...going twice...gone! Sold to Signor Arnold, ladies and gentlemen, at a record price for the day, I might add!" declared the auctioneer, Roberto, an elegant 80-year-old of small stature but with a voice of lion. "And with that, the auction is concluded. Thank you for coming."

Fantastic applause roars through the air, but in spite of all that noise, I could not hear a thing. I could only feel the tears forming in my eyes.

"Father, you did it! You sold it. One Hundred and seventy million pounds," my Juliette whispers in my ear.

"We said seventy-five schools this morning. Now, it's 250, Juliette, 250!" I replied, pulling my daughter into a happy embrace.

Chapter One

My sister Catherin and I sat just outside the dimly lit bedroom, with our ears pressed firmly against the door. I could make out some of what was being said, and I could clearly hear my mother's faint crying as she sat by my grandfather's bedside. He had been bedridden for the last ten tiring days, and even at just 10 years old, I understood what a harsh reality death was. I also knew my grandfather was close to it. A few hours earlier, Mother had taken my sister and me in the room to say our farewells. We just kissed him and said a few words, and he didn't even respond. Truly, it was a sad demise for a man who'd spent his life as such a flamboyant soul.

Dr. Jacques, our grumpy and bold but helpful neighbor, had been stopping by for the last week or so. He was a faithful friend to our grandfather for decades, despite being fourteen years his junior. They loved sharing a smoke on the balcony and had been doing so for as long as I could recall. I would never forget my grandfather smoking his brown, wooden pipe with the golden handle and Dr. Jacques taking puffs from his black pipe with the steel handle, for it was their ritual every evening until my grandfather took ill.

Dr. Jacques was visiting again, dressed in a plain, white shirt and blue trousers. He stuck around for a few hours after our farewell, and when the door finally opened, he followed my mother out and closed the door behind them. My mother, so emotionally overwhelmed, couldn't bear to utter a word, so she went straight to her room. Dr. Jacques was sweating profusely when he knelt down and, in a low, sad voice told us our grandfather had died.

The next day, my grandfather was buried in Père Lachaise Cemetery, about fifteen minutes away. Over a hundred came to pay their respects, despite the soaking, heavy rain on that March morning in 1956.

My own father died very young, taken from us by tuberculosis, so my grandfather was a father to me and more. He loved sharing his life stories with us, and he was passionate about art, reading, and traveling. Listening to him inspired me at an early age, but one story in particular changed my life. He must have talked about his alleged meeting with the great Victor Hugo a dozen times. My mother never really believed it, but deep inside, I felt he was telling the truth.

Just past noon on a summer day in 1877, my great-grandmother asked my grandfather, just 6 at the time, to run an errand near their home in Place des Vosges, in the Marais District, between the third and fourth arrondissements of Paris. She was cooking lunch for a family friend visiting from Bordeaux, and she was none too happy to discover that my mother's uncle, my grandfather's younger brother, had nibbled on the bread she'd held back for the meal. It would be far too embarrassing, after all, to serve bread with little bite marks in it here and there. My mother's uncle was penalized with a slap on his hand, and my grandfather was ordered to the nearby bakery to get a fresh loaf. "Come back as fast as lightning now!" his mother demanded.

After my grandfather luckily purchased the last loaf at the bakery, he headed home. On his way, he noticed a small but striking white cat with a golden collar. Like most boys his age, he couldn't resist the temptation to follow the animal, and it led him to the gardens of the Hotel de Sully. The foliage and orchards were majestic, a wide array of roses and flowers bursting with all imaginable colors. It was spectacularly landscaped, in a fashion worthy of one of the most important buildings built in Paris in the seventeenth century by famous architect Jean Androuet du Cerceau.

My grandfather wasted a few minutes looking anxiously for the cat, but there was no sign of the wayward pet. He glanced up at the sky and remembered that the hour was growing late and that his impatient mother would have a fit if he ruined her lunch by not returning with the bread in a hurry. With that on his mind, he ran as fast as his young legs would carry him.

As he took a sharp turn in the artistic labyrinth of lovely gardens, he bumped into an old man; in fact, he collided so hard with the stranger that he knocked some paper and a big, green apple out of his hands. The man helped the boy up. My grandfather was about to apologize to the elder one with the strange hat when he recognized that he'd crashed into none other than Victor Hugo, one of the most prominent figures in Paris, a great writer and a man of infinite knowledge, the living legend behind one of his favorite stories, *The Hunchback of Notre Dame*. Of course, Victor Hugo was also known as a man of outspoken opinion and temper. My grandfather recalled that just staring into his eyes made him shiver and tied his tongue, so he could not say a word.

Surprisingly, Victor Hugo boasted an unexpected smile and said, "You must be saving us from the Prussian army, running like that, young boy."

"I am sorry, really sorry, but my mother will kill me if I don't get this bread back in time. We have a guest, and lunch must be served soon," my grandfather replied, all fear gone in the wake of the man's generous smile.

"Tell your mother, patience. As long as there is food, everyone will eat in the end. Tell her Victor Hugo made Napoleon wait for an hour one day, yet here I am, alive and well! Run along, boy. *Au revoir,*" the great man said before he retrieved his apple from the ground and made his way to one of the benches to eat it.

That encounter, true or not, had been proudly retold for generations. "Can you believe that happened to me? The hat, the smile, the green apple..." he told the doubters, always punctuating his tale with a big chuckle.

After my grandfather passed away, the encounter he talked about ran through my head a hundred times. As a result, I became obsessed with Hugo's work, and that whetted my appetite for the writings of other greats. I visited museums and exhibitions all over France, sat down in countless libraries and buried my nose in books, old scrolls, and manuscripts. Poring over that historical literature piqued my interest in other things, and I began to develop a passion for art, paintings, and sculpture. From an early age, I knew exactly where I'd end up one day.

I was lucky enough to be brought up in a household that could afford to support my many ventures, thanks to my grandfather, who'd done well for himself in life. After his literal collision with the great Victor Hugo, he also fell in love with literature, plays, and the opera. After graduating from Sorbonne University with high marks in English language and literature, he opened a small library of his own for a few years. He knew there was a shortage of printing presses, for many books— English ones in particular—were too quickly out of print. Those produced by small publishers were rare and difficult to find; sometimes it took several months to get new additions. So, he started his own company and gave it his family name, Russeau, with intent to target the suppliers of foreign books. His place started as a small company, but it grew and grew as he built a strong reputation among his peers through his hard work and dedication.

Later in life, he married his neighbor's daughter, my late grandmother, Sophie. "One of the most beautiful women in all of Paris," my grandfather and mother used to say about her, and that was proven by the photographs of her. Truly, she was a work of art all her own.

Things were going great for them, until first word of war came to them. In his forties, my grandfather was called to serve in the army reserves. When his unit was mobilized, he found himself involved in the war, based in the Alsace-Lorraine region. My grandmother and my mother were left alone in Paris, and they lived off the money earned by the company before it was forced to close down for several years in my grandfather's absence. When the war ended, he came back to resume his work, but it took another decade to put the business back in order. Nevertheless, his efforts reaped some success once more, till World War II interrupted their lives and the Nazis took over Paris.

My father, a worker at the printing press, met my mother one day when she came to walk her father home. They spent a few years getting to know one another before they married, back in 1935. For a long while, they tried to have children, only to be disappointed. Then, when World War II erupted, my father enlisted in the French army.

Dad's regiment suffered huge defeats at the cruel hands of the advancing, merciless Nazis. He luckily survived, only to be imprisoned for three years in Dresden in Germany. During his absence, my grandfather had to manage the press alone. Even worse, the place was closed several times by the Nazis, with accusations of spreading anti-Nazi propaganda, for Paris was flooded with leaflets encouraging the French resistance. When it was proven that none of the accusations were sound, the facility reopened, but the damage had been done. Business was scarce during that poverty epidemic. Life was miserable for everyone then, and my grandparents were not immune to the suffering. In fact, they barely survived those difficult days under the oppressive Nazi occupation.

When the allies finally secured victory, my father returned. Of course, he was not the same man; he died inside while he was jailed and tortured by those devils. Miraculously, my parents were blessed with two kids, me first and my sister two years later. The blessing stopped there though.

Three years after the war, my father met his end when he just fell asleep and never woke up. A week later, my grandmother Sophie joined him, leaving my mother, my sister, and me to rely on the old man. My mother sold the flat I'd grown up in, and we all moved into my grandfather's place, a cozy three-bedroom apartment on the second floor of a eighteenth-century, three-story building. There were two flats on each floor, and we shared our floor with Dr. Jacques, who lived alone.

At first, it was very hard for all of us to adjust, but under the guidance of my grandfather and through her own strong will, my mother gradually took over for her old man, and we managed to move on. We kids kept busy with school, and in the summers, we played with the other neighborhood children or ran around the printing press, fascinated by all those loud machines.

The facility was just over 2,000 square feet. It occupied the whole ground floor of a small, two-story building within the Latin Quarter, just two streets away from the beautiful Pantheon. Four workers were managed by my mother, under the supervision of my grandfather. In his later days, the old man took it easy. He often only worked half-days and spent the rest of his time entertaining us. He loved to take us to the Jardin du Luxembourg garden, where we played around the fountain and floated our toy wooden boats while he read his books. On the cold, rainy days, we spent our days at home with him; he loved telling us stories of his war days as he cooked lunch for us, and more than once, he told us his tale of the day he met Victor Hugo.

"The man of *The Hunchback of Notre Dame*?" I asked.

"Always mention *Les Misérables* first, Sebastian," Grandfather always answered.

After his death, the work and burden of handling it all on her own became a bit tiring for her. The machines did not function as well, for they were old and worn out, in need of costly repairs. Mother had no choice but to sell the press to a bigger company, but she was offered a good price. I studied history, but Catherin was more interested in love; she married a young businessman who had just started a goldmining company in South Africa. A few years later, she gave birth to twin girls, and she rarely came back to Paris.

I loved my days at the university. I was fulfilling my dream of learning more about history and culture, and my adoration of it reflected in my studies, as I excelled in every subject. I knew I was fortunate to be sent to Greece and Iraq for a month with three other students during my last year, as part of a German-French delegation sent to study historical sites. I loved learning about the Greeks, but I was even more interested in the Assyrians. Visiting Athens and Mosul was the climax of that trip. It was enthralling for me to see firsthand what humanity had achieved thousands and thousands years ago, with so few resources.

I easily landed a job in the library at the Louvre after my studies. There, I was surrounded by sculpture, paintings, and manmade wonders, and I enjoyed every minute of my job. I was the first there in the morning and didn't mind leaving hours after my shift, as long as I got home in time to enjoy one of my mother's home-cooked meals and a glass or two of the finest red wine. Our living area, that little haven of ours, was lovingly adorned with its own beauty, small landscape paintings, carpets, and sculptures. My mother and work were my life back then, and I was my mother's world. Every night, she was eager to hear every detail about my day at The Louvre. Through our talks, she became more knowledgeable than most when it came to history. She also visited the museum a few times a month, and she never missed a special exhibition. Often, our chatter kept us up till just before midnight, and only then would she gently excuse herself and go to bed.

Mom always fell asleep within minutes, but I always stayed up to wash the dishes. Afterward, I poured myself another glass of wine and sat in the black rocking chair in the corner of our living room, the same chair my grandfather occupied for years. I loved to turn down the overhead lights and just read by the dim flickering of a six-candle candelabra. I loved that welcoming corner of the living room more than any spot in the house; there was just something endearing about it: the beautiful dark brown corner table with a silky, golden cloth half-covering it; the small, colorful Herend porcelain hummingbird statue; and the lovely bohemian crystal ashtray at my side. There were so many delicate treasures there, things my grandfather had purchased during his world travels.

In that little corner, I immersed myself in books about artists, not only about their work but also diaries and biographies, stories about their personal lives. Our museum library was rich with such books, and I thoroughly enjoyed them. One day, I was living in the world of Van Gogh. The next, I was in Manet's domain. If I was not in the mood for reading, I just picked up my guitar, a birthday gift from my sister several years prior. Throughout the years, I learned to master the instrument, and I loved to practice the few songs I knew. When I tired of reading or playing, I blew out the candles and headed to my bed for six or so hours of sleep.

On workdays, I woke up early to bathe and enjoy a cup of coffee, fresh brewed by my mother, who was always up around six a.m. She liked to brew the coffee slowly, as she read the daily paper, and she always prepared a sandwich for me to take for my lunch. That was our daily routine during the week, but we did things a bit differently on the weekends.

On Friday nights, I often joined some friends at a small bar in Saint German. My mother invited her two best friends, Mrs. Susanne and Mrs. Claudia, over. The women were both in their early sixties, widows and retired school teachers. The ladies spent their Friday evenings talking, drinking, and smoking dainty little cigarettes that were carefully packed in their handcrafted silver boxes with their initials engraved on them.

After six years of working in the museum library, I was promoted to head one of the treasury storage rooms. While the museum proudly put many items on display, just as many precious artifacts were stored securely, not visible to the public. These were very protected items, kept in controlled temperatures and under dim lighting. Each piece was carefully covered and only uncovered to be cleaned from time to time.

Every now and then, some paintings from the permanent displays were removed or sent to other museums temporarily, so some of the paintings from the stock rooms were put in their place. It was an amazing experience being able to hold history in my bare hands. The feeling was beyond explanation when I was asked one day to carry one of Van Gogh's painting to the cleaning department. This happened again and again, and I was privileged to lay my hands on the works of many other great artists.

As the weeks passed, I began to learn more about the things in storage and those on display. I was taught how to carefully handle those treasures, how to treat them with the respect they deserved, how to clean and maintain those beauties so generations ahead could view them the same way our ancestors did. Every detail was important in our work, from the type of gloves we wore to the brushes we used to the proper packaging to the step-by-step instructions when moving any pieces from one place to another. There were protocols in place regarding what we wore: head covers were required in the storage areas, so no wayward strands of hair would contaminate anything. Cigarettes, matches, and any spray of any kind—whether it was asthma medicine or hairspray—were strictly forbidden. Since no food or drinks were allowed inside, we took shifts for lunch and midday breaks.

All rules were strictly followed, and Professor Schmidt could not afford to give anyone a second chance for even the slightest mistake or oversight. When it came to those invaluable pieces of art, one mess-up was one too many. Anyone who made an error was lucky to be moved to another division; most were excused from that museum and blacklisted from working in any museums in France. Negligence simply was not tolerated. Everyone held the professor in high regard, rightfully so. Schmidt had worked in The Louvre for thirty-eight years, since several years before World War II. He was from Darmstadt, in the southwest part of Germany, just outside Frankfurt. He had a doctorate in arts preservation from the Sorbonne University, the same school my grandfather attended. He moved to France at the age of 18 and never returned. It was said that The Louvre wouldn't have been the same museum it was without him. Schmidt's negotiations, tactics, and cunning got the better of the Nazis. When necessary, he hid important paintings from the invaders. Other times, he cleverly tricked them into taking fakes. He used every trick in the book to protect the real treasures. Yes, The Louvre gave up some of its precious jewels as casualties of war, but if not for Professor Schmidt, those losses would have numbered hundreds more. He was a legend, and I considered it a privilege to work under him.

His reputation seemed bigger than the man himself. Really, the professor was just a tiny man with a long chin, pearl-white teeth, and ears that seemed too big for his head. Above his eyes was a unibrow, but despite his age, there wasn't a white hair in his head. He was clean shaven always, and he could drill a hole in anyone with his light green eyes. He seemed to see all things, and no one would dare try to do anything under his nose, for he watched every move everyone made. He walked with the aid of a long cane, and he only had to hit the floor with it twice to still everyone in the area.

When I was there, Professor Schmidt had two years left to work at the museum. He was very generous with his knowledge, willing to pass it on to all who would listen. He even gained the approval of the board members to give a weekly two-hour lecture about art preservation and authentication. Those presentations were offered at eleven a.m. on Saturdays. An average of forty-five people attended every week. The majority were first timers, trainees, students of art from all over the region, and employees. Most employees chose to only attend once a month, but eight showed up in Hall D every week to hear him, and of course I was one of them.

After hitting the floor twice with his cane, the professor turned to write something on the board in big, bold letters, "Temperature and light." He then turned to us and elaborated, "Those are the two worst enemies, as well as the best friends, of any artwork. Always remember that. If any artwork is preserved at the optimal temperature, it will live forever. If exposed to perfect, safe lighting, it will show its beauty off even to those blind to art. On the other hand, if it is exposed to temperatures too high or too low, the jewel will be killed. If the lighting is too bright, you may as well saturate the art with water or bring a pencil or hammer and make your own art of it. In the wrong light and temperature, the irreplaceable works of masters like Van Gogh, Monet, or Cezanne will lose their beauty, lose the awe they inspire in us all. Temperature and light. Remember that!" the old man shouted, tapping each word on the board with the butt of his cane.

That first lecture lasted only thirty minutes, but it earned him a standing ovation, and I was hooked right there.

Months later, Professor Schmidt borrowed a piece from storage and explained all the basics of handling it. His lectures became more interesting, more intense, sometimes stretching into three hours. Word spread about those sessions, and he soon began receiving invitations from all over Europe, imploring him to speak to the masses.

As time went on, I strived to be closer to the man, for I respected him greatly and tried to devour all the knowledge he shared. In return, the professor admired my passion and felt I was his prodigy. "Your grandfather would have been proud of you, Sebastian," he told me on several occasions.

Professor Schmidt eventually invited me to accompany him during his travels. Most often, we left on Friday evenings and returned to Paris late on Sundays. It was a hectic time but a rich, cultural experience. We visited Berlin, Zurich, Amsterdam, Vienna, Brussels, London, and many other places. He advised me to invest more in myself, I decided to heed his advice and spent some of my hard-earned income on courses and exchange programs during the first year with him.

During his fiftieth lecture, the professor entered wearing a colorful red shirt and loose, white trousers, a far cry different from his usual dark suit and crisp, white shirt. He stood in the middle of the room, which was odd as well, since he usually stood at the front. He then hit the floor with his cane three times and said, "Today, I will speak about something even more important than preserving the lovely jewels we have been talking about for my past forty-nine lectures. Today, we will learn how to distinguish a real jewel from a fake, a real painting from one created by an imposter, a sculpture crafted by a great rather than one carved by mere apprentice. Some of these reproductions may be splendid masterpieces in their own right, but they are not the works of the masters' hands. Today, we will learn about the authentication of art." With that, he made his way to the chalkboard and wrote, in bold letters, "AOA." Then he turned to the crowd, wearing a big smile, and said, "I do believe this abbreviation will do for now." Once he returned to the middle of the room, he continued, "Our committee, like other AOA companies and panels, consists of researchers, scientists, and various technical experts. During my sixteen years on the museum AOA committee, we have authenticated 186 pieces of art. Out of that lot, nineteen turned out to be fakes. Remember that number, nineteen. Millions of dollars, francs, or pounds could have been lost if we had overlooked any of those, and the scammers would have become rich at the world's expense.

"A golden rule you must all follow, one you won't likely find in any book, is that you must always pay attention to your first impression. Never underestimate that. Out of the nineteen we ultimately discovered, I could immediately tell that twleve were knock-offs, within the first twenty seconds." He paused to smile at the crowd, smirked a little, then continued, "Now, perhaps you think this old man is making this up. If you do, feel free to ask around. Some of those who were on that committee still work here, at the museum. How did I know though? Well, a few days before the work was presented to us, we were given a brief to study. I learned as much as I could about the artists behind the work, literally spent hours investigating those creators. I perused every source I could find, learning the artists' techniques. Was the painter right- or left-handed? What colors did he prefer to mix? What about his signature, the position of it? I absorbed every small detail, so that when I looked at those works, I knew, without any shadow of doubt, whether or not the suggested artist was the creator of it." He then paused and said, "For the sake of a practical example of first impressions and instant observation, is there anything anyone would like to point out about today's lecture?"

I was about to raise my hand when a lady sitting in the front beat me to it.

"Yes, Ana, isn't it?" Professor Schmidt asked, pointing at her with his cane.

The girl nodded.

"We shared a smoke a few weeks back on the terrace, on the last floor, did we not?" he continued.

Again, Ana nodded again.

"You have been coming here for the last three weeks. Go ahead, modern lady," he said with a smile.

His observations of the student were definitely correct; she was very modern in her attire, from her tight clothes to her top that only covered one shoulder. She accessorized that look with a bright pink scarf, and her rather short black hair had two different colors in the back, one strand of blonde and another of red.

"You are wearing red, and…"

As soon as she paused, I cut in, "And you are not wearing a jacket today. Not only that, but—"

This time, Ana interrupted me, glaring at me and boldly finishing, "You are standing in the middle of the room, not at the front."

"Yes, and you hit the ground three times with your cane, Professor, not two," I said, even more loudly than before, as if we were in a shouting competition.

"Wow! Look at them go. I love this. You are like two authentication houses. Ladies and gentlemen, this is your proof about first impressions. These two have done their homework, learning about me and the surroundings well. I would guess that within minutes of arriving in this class today, they felt something was out of the ordinary. If I had come in wearing red for weeks or months, they would not have noticed.

Details, my friends. Always observe and study the details, and you will find your answers there."

He dismissed us early that day, with two bangs of his cane on the floor. Before we departed, the whole class broke into applause. I, however, was focused on something else, staring shamelessly at the mysterious lady. I hadn't seen her before, which I assumed was because I'd missed the last three of the professor's lectures while I was busy in Florence and Pisa in the Tuscan region of Italy.

At first, Ana did not turn to look at me again, but once she was on her feet, she did. When our eyes met for the first time, it was a quick glance but a deep one. In fact, I was sure that stare would have continued longer if the professor didn't speak again.

"Next week, we will discuss the other seven works, which required more than instincts. See you then."

That day, a new phase in my life began, and Ana was to become an integral part of it.

Chapter Two

I Looked at my watch and was glad to see that the professor had let us out early. It was truly the right thing to do after such a heavy, heated discussion, a condensed lecture jam-packed with information. The weather was lovely, so I decided to walk to the café right outside the Opera Garnier, to join my two close friends for lunch. I had known Antoine and Émilie since I was 12, and we'd been best friends ever since, even after the two of them married a few years back. They were a fine example of a lasting school-age crush, and they made a wonderful couple. Antoine worked as a journalist for a local newspaper, and Émilie was a professional photographer who took snaps of models, actors, and athletes for various advertisements through her PR agency. The two of them lived on a beautiful loft on rue Rivoli, close to where I worked, so we got together every once in a while.

To my surprise, I found both of them prompt and already sitting at our regular table, right next to the window that overlooked the architectural masterpiece of the opera. They were bickering about something, as usual. The closer I got to them, the smaller I felt; both of them towered at least five inches over my six feet. I smiled at my friends as I approached the table.

Émilie holding a cigarette, was wearing a short, white dress adorned here and there with a rose pattern. Her

that Ana dropping in on lunch was as much a surprise to me as it was to them.

"To be honest, I've never even seen Sebastian before, not till he interrupted me today." She turned to me and continued, "I hope I didn't scratch your ego in class. Truth be told, I followed you here to make sure I didn't hurt your feelings," she said as she smiled and gave me a pat on the back.

"I... Well, I-I..." I stuttered.

"Just joking," she said, her smile broadening. She then turned back to Émilie. "I like your friend's confidence, and I find him...interesting. This time, she broke into a laugh as she looked me directly in the eye.

"I like this one, however he found her," Émilie whispered to Antoine, so loudly that we all heard her.

"Do you fancy some red wine, Ana?" Émilie asked.

Ana nodded. "Absolutely."

"Philippe, cancel my Perrier. Sparkling water will do us no good. Please bring your best Bordeaux, with two glasses," Émilie corrected.

"Make that three" Antoine said.

"Wow. This has been the fastest two minutes of my life. What just happened?" I asked.

Émilie gave me a wink and a thumbs-up as I gawked at her with a puzzled look on my face.

Three hours later, we had finished four bottles of wine. Not only that, but Ana and I had shared our first kiss. I had never encountered such a soul before; she was full of energy, like a ball of fire.

In the days that followed, Ana and I spent our breaks together whenever we could. Twice after work, we met in that same café and were joined by Émilie and Antoine. By the time Professor Schmidt presented his next lecture, I knew all there was to know about Ana, and she knew just as much about me.

I learned that Ana had moved to Paris several months prior, from Strasbourg. She was 22, making her 7 years my junior and the youngest of four sisters. She was a bit of a latecomer for her parents, for her closest sister was twelve years older. Her father was the owner of a lumber factory, and he considered himself a Strasbourg man of German origin. Her mother, on the other hand, considered herself French. Two of Ana's sisters married Italian men who worked with her father, and her eldest sister married a Swiss banker and moved to Zurich.

"I consider myself a citizen of the world. There are three languages spoken fluently in my house. It is like a circus. You ask in French, someone answers in

Alsatian, you reply in Alsatian, and they answer in Italian," she explained with a laugh.

She told me that she dropped out of school at the age of 16 and dedicated her time to her artwork. She attended private classes taught by an expressionist artist in the Alsace region. She showed us some of her work, and it was as unique as she was. Ana was a real talent. Most of her drawings were from the art dipping movement, and red was her color of choice; various hues and mixtures of crimson shades were a common theme in the oil colors she showed us. They were stunning, so it wasn't surprising to hear that one of her teachers had pulled some strings to land her there in Paris, to work at The Louvre.

"I won't be here long. It's just a learning phase, to broaden my vision," she said.

I knew much about art, but I was as far away as anyone could be from being an actual artist. Even my handwriting was horrible. Ana was the opposite, artistic in every way possible. For us, it was a case of opposites attracting, and our mutual attraction was obvious to anyone who knew us at the time. We did share some commonalities, such as a love for dancing and a passion for jazz in particular.

We enjoyed our first real date just five days after our first encounter. On that clear Friday night, I wore dark jeans and a white and black checkered, long-sleeved shirt. I rode my bicycle to her place.

At the time, Ana was sharing a flat with two other girls who were also interested in art. I waited for a few minutes before she came down and nearly took my breath away in her short, blue skirt and sleeveless, white satin top. She strutted down in blue high heels. Her hair was combed over to the left side, exposing her soft right cheek and the pearl earring in that ear. Again, she donned that sheen of light pink lipstick, and her fingernails matched that shade this time. She smiled when she saw me and leaned over so I could place a gentle kiss on her right cheek; when I did, I caught a whiff of her strong perfume, a scent that reminded me of a delicious mix of vanilla and coffee.

"Like it?" Ana asked.

I answered with another kiss planted on her neck, and I inhaled her aroma once more from that soft place.

The jazz place wasn't too crowded when we got there, but within an hour, it was packed. The band picked up the tempo and took it to the next level. People filled the stage, but it was clear which couple owned it. There was no doubt that it was our night to conquer.

The next day, Professor Schmidt showed up in his normal dark, pinstriped suit and starched white shirt. This time, though, I sat next to Ana, in the second row.

When the cane hit the floor twice, the class went silent. Over sixty people were present this time.

"Seven difficult fakes. Remember? Out of the nineteen we caught over the years, seven pushed us to the limit. For those who missed our previous lecture, this was what we were speaking about. Speaking of that rather...heated lecture, I see that our two houses, Sebastian and Ana, are sitting next to one another this time. Last week, you were ready to devour one another with your glares and words. Perhaps you are trying to heed that old adage, to keep your friends close but your enemies closer, no?"

"Friends, Professor," we both replied at the same time.

The whole class laughed for a moment, till the cane struck twice and silence resumed.

"Let me paint a clear picture for you all in regard to how we did our job. The piece at stake was placed between us. Each of us was equipped with a magnifying glass, a small notebook, and a pencil. We gathered around the work and took turns taking a closer look. Some scribbled a few notes and returned to scrutinize the art once again, often several times.

After an hour, we met to discuss our findings. Do you all understand the process?" Professor Schmidt asked.

We all nodded.

"Good," he continued. "Now, for those doubtable seven, we relied on a mixture of science and knowledge. We used scientific methods to determine the age of materials, as well as features hidden to the naked eye. We then compared those discoveries with all the information we had on the original artists. Those scientific methods included the use of a stereoscopic microscope, which uses light reflected from the surface of an object rather than transmitted through it. This helped us determine the pigments (crystallinity, its size or purity), as well as the nature of the craquelure (deep or superficial-natural or artificial), restoration, and other factors related to the age of the paints. We found discrepancies in most of the seven fakes.

"Another scientific method we used was black light. Now, this requires much study, but I will put it to you as simply as possible. Different surfaces, colors, and materials react differently to black light. This helps us to detect inconsistency. A simple example that led us to determine that one of the seven were fake was the signature. After applying the black light—or a wooden lamp light, as others might call it—to the whole painting, we noticed differences in the lower left corner where the signature was, discrepancies between glowing and black colors. That was all the proof we needed that the signature was added after the varnish was applied to the whole painting. That would have been highly contrary to common pattern of the artist, as he was known to apply varnish years after signing his own work. Digging a bit deeper into the work revealed that some parts of the painting were at least fifty years more recent than his death, so we knew he couldn't possibly have painted it.

"Another method we've used more recently is called infrared reflectography (IRR), invented just over a decade ago by a Dutch physicist. I had the pleasure of meeting J.R.J. van Asperen De Boer years ago at a lecture. His method requires us to peer through the paint layers. It is a bit similar to x-radiography, except that it reveals slightly different information. When the longer wavelengths of infrared radiation penetrate the paint layers, the upper layers appear transparent. The degree of penetration depends on the thickness of the paint, the type of paint, and the length of the wave of infrared radiation. The longer the wavelength of the infrared and the thinner the paint layers, the easier it is to penetrate to the layers beneath. Many paints appear partially or completely transparent under infrared, while others, such as black, will absorb the infrared radiation and appear dark. The contrast of absorption of various materials reveals layers of the painting not visible to the naked eye, such as the underdrawings and changes in the paint layers.

"It is important to note a particular point here," the professor went on. "Unless the artist himself delivers the work face to face and signs to swear that the work is his, there is no need for any authentication. Unfortunately, as most artists of these precious works are no longer with us, the rising of the dead would be the requirement to avoid the hassle. For this reason, authentication of art is a necessary process much of the time.

"Certainly you have all heard of or seen the *Mona Lisa*, *La Gioconda*, the painting by Leonardo Di Vinci. Is there anyone here who hasn't?" the professor asked.

No one dared to reply to that.

"Great, for if any hands were raised, I would have to ask you to leave my lecture posthaste!" he said boisterously. "Are any of you aware that it was stolen on a hot, humid day in 1911, on August 21?"

For an answer, a few gasps erupted across the rows, and eyes grew wide.

"I find it interesting that many have no knowledge of this. The lovely *Mona Lisa* went missing for more than two years, courtesy of an Italian who once worked here in The Louvre, Vincenzo Perugia. The whole incident made worldwide news in every major city, and a remarkable reward of around 500,000 francs was offered to anyone who could provide useful information that would lead to the return of

Leonardo's masterpiece. People from all over the world provided information, a few fakes were brought forward, and interrogations ensued. Even Picasso was questioned, along with his once close friend, the avant-garde poet and playwright Guillaume Apollinaire. The two went at each other, desperate to clear their names. Of course they were both innocent, but they were acquainted with a witty Belgian who'd been guilty of some mischief in the past. Picasso and Apollinaire supposedly never spoke again. Anyway, you can read more about that after the lecture.

"What is important for us today is to remember that weeks upon weeks of tests and research had to be undergone on the recovered *Mona Lisa*, till it was officially declared authentic. It was said that many AOA from all over the world provided free assistance. Again, it is a reminder why every piece must be carefully inspected and certified. I realize this is a lot of information, but this hour of difficult scientific jargon and some basic knowledge will do you a world of good. Surely my years and years of study and all the hard work I went through to bring you this information should get a clap, should it not?" Professor Schmidt concluded, bludgeoning the floor twice more with his cane.

I had attended most of Professor Schmidt's lectures at The Louvre, and several in other places. They were all deep and interesting for art aficionados, but that was his best so far. I was the first to offer him a standing ovation, with Ana right behind me, and then the whole class, offering their loud applause.

As Professor Schmidt grinned from ear to ear and bowed like a maestro, Ana put her hand on mine. "You will be like him one day. Remember I told you so!"

It had been nearly two years since I was promoted to head of one of the treasury stores and a few months since I was asked to join the AOA committee. I had the privilege of working directly under Professor Schmidt, and I learned so much from him. Everything is meant to come to an end at some point, though, and now, the professor was facing retirement in two weeks, as he'd reached the age of 62. The museum planned a great farewell party for the man who had given so much to the place. The gathering was to be held in one of the halls of the Grand Palais, and over 200 people were invited. It would be a fitting send-off for a wise and good man.

My mother had met the professor several times and insisted on inviting him over for dinner before he departed for his hometown in Darmstadt, Germany. We welcomed him on a Saturday night, and she expertly prepared a whole chicken stuffed with rice, potatoes, and small carrots, slowly cooked for hours in the stove with her secret gravy, full of a mystery mix of savory spices. The professor repeatedly praised the meal, and I had to join him in that. Before that night, she asked me what type of food Professor Schmidt liked most; fortunately, through my many trips with him, I learned that he loved chicken more than anything else. The rest was up to her, and she made an unforgettable feast that our guest enjoyed.

During our hours together that evening, the professor explained that he planned to spend the whole summer back in Germany, to his birthplace, Darmstadt. He wanted to learn more about a myth concerning the castle of Frankenstein, then return to Paris. "I consider it home here," he said, "and I am looking forward to daily walks and reading as many books as I can."

Once he returned to Paris several months later, I met him from time to time for a drink, sometimes alone and sometimes with Ana on my arm.

Ana and I had been together for a year, the longest of any of my relationships. The three I'd had in the past never lasted longer than a month. Things were different with Ana though. With us, there was no pressure. We were extremely happy and enjoyed the time we spent together. The relationship was going in all directions, which we were well aware of. We also knew that we couldn't think too much about going forward or committing. We had to live for the here and now, so that was what we did.

I needed Ana, for she came into my life at a time when I'd begun to isolate myself from most of my surroundings. I was so obsessed with art that I'd begun to see little else. She loosened me up, showed me that life could be a healthy mixture of freedom and art.

On the other hand, I was what Ana needed as well. I balanced her craziness with a little simplicity, and I was all the support she needed for her work. I pushed her to higher limits, helped her to believe more in her work, and that came through in her art expression.

We weren't the kind of couple who sat down for candlelight dinners or planned romantic nights out. Everything just happened naturally between us. Sometimes, I asked Ana to join me at home for a quick drink with my mother. Other times, Ana called at nightfall, and I would make a cheese plate, grab a bottle of wine from a nearby store, fling my guitar over my shoulder, and ride my bicycle to Pont Marie. There, Ana would be waiting for me, dressed comfortably in jeans and a loose top, with her hair tied behind her head. We spent many nights sitting on the banks of the River Seine, enjoying the reflection of the moonlight off the water, watching the boats slowly float back and forth. We enjoyed just being together, and she seemed to love the tunes I picked out on my guitar.

Once in a while, I would hear a noise against my window late at night. When I peeked out to see what it was, there was Ana, waiting for me with a smile on her face. I loved to join her for those long, moonlit walks. Those happened more frequently after Ana quit her job at the museum. She had managed to sell a few of her paintings for just over 4,000 francs, enough to cover her expenses for three or four months. Because she wasn't working for eight hours in a museum, she could focus more on producing art. She'd benefitted greatly from her time at The Louvre, though, and once she felt she gleaned all the knowledge she could from it, it was time for her to move on.

One night when she showed up below, I joined her again, just as I had on many other nights. It was chilly, so after we walked for ten minutes, we decided to stop at a bar to warm up. We shared a small bite and had a few drinks, enough to leave us feeling a little tipsy when we left. Halfway back, we were pelted by a vicious rainstorm, such a downpour that it felt as if someone was throwing buckets of water on us. We ran as fast as we could, laughing hysterically, until we reached her place. She dried her hair and offered me her red bathrobe to wear while my clothes dried. Fortunately, her two roommates were out of town; otherwise, I never could have shown my face again, walking around with soaked hair, in a woman's robe.

The girls shared a very large, colorful living room. It was furnished with a black sofa large enough for two, a rather small, white table topped with several ashtrays, and a bigger red table near the window, home to a small cactus and a funky record player. It was obvious that the boarders used the place as an art studio, for three small, round chairs and a dozen canvases lay next to one of the walls. Water and oil color tubes were thrown here and there, along with brushes of different types and sizes and several palettes. Not only that, but there was the tell-tale aroma of paint wafting from every corner.

I took a seat on one of the small chairs and watched as the rain splattered against the window. When Ana came in and handed me one of the coffee mugs she was carrying, then sat on the floor beside me, we exchanged looks for a few minutes.

"Take it off," she said, gazing up at me from under her wet bangs. "The robe."

"Feeling wild?" I asked.

"Please just take it off, Sebastian. And then, don't move."

A bit confused, I did as she said. I stared at her for a second before it dawned on me. "Oh! You want to draw me, Ana?"

"Turn to the right. I want to see that half of you, only your profile. Just keep looking out the window, like you were a moment ago."

Again, I did as she said.

"Perfect! Just like that," Ana said, but then she paused and moved nearer. "Is this okay? I mean, would you rather do it another day?" she asked, so close that her damp hair sent a chill across my skin.

"Now is fine, baby. I am all yours. I feel it, can see it in your eyes. Draw me...right now," I said.

"All mine? I do hope you mean that, Sebastian. I want to do something new with this. I hope you trust me," she said, with great determination in her voice.

"Trust you?" I questioned, looking at her a bit suspiciously. "Okay, this is getting weird now," I said as I stood and kissed both her hands.

"I want to soak you in red, then paint you," she confessed. "It will take only two hours, three at the most. If you'll do this for me, I promise to make it up to you one day. Please?" she begged, then planted a tender kiss on my neck.

"I would never get in the way of real art," I said. "I was just soaked to the bone by buckets of cold rain. I don't think having red paint spilled on me could be much worse. Let us do this." I said.

It took nearly forty-five minutes to set up the place, to cover everything so nothing would be ruined or messed up and Ana wouldn't have to answer to her roommates upon their return. We spread old newspapers on the floor, creating a trail of them from the bathtub to the small chair I would sit in, so I could look out the window. Of course the chair was wrapped with paper as well.

The whole setup was raw art itself. I could feel adrenaline pumping in my veins. I was happy to be a model for the first time, especially since I was modeling for an artist I admired, a person I was sure had a future in the demanding world of art.

Ana handed me some goggles to wear before the great red dip. She also gave me cotton balls to shove in my hears. We each took two fast shots from her bottle of tequila, and then we were ready for our little adventure.

The bathtub was filled with watered-down red paint. *It looks like a crime scene,* I thought, *but what the hell?* I took a deep breath and, carefully and with Ana's help, stepped in. I was most grateful that she'd used warm water. While I'd never been a religious person of any sort, it felt as if I was being baptized, as if I was taking part in some sort of commitment ceremony to be holy artistic at higher levels from that point forward.

After every part of me was covered, Ana guided me back, steering my naked, red body to the chair. She allowed me a couple sips of water from a bottle so I could spit out the red paint that had crept into my mouth. Next, she walked over to the record player and put on a vinyl of Spanish guitar music. She danced all around me, clearly feeling the beat. Carefully, she removed the goggles from my face, then placed her chair ten feet away from me. She sat down in front of her thirty-by-thirty-six-inch canvas and started her magic.

As the music played, her brushstrokes responded continuously. My neck began to ache after twenty minutes, and I felt some pain in my shoulders, but I seemed to get used to it after a while. Ignoring the stiffness in my muscles and the feeling of paint drying on my skin, I just closed my eyes and let that music carry me away, just as it was doing to her. We stopped several times so I could stand to stretch, but she was always quickly back to work. We rarely talked for the three hours she worked, but there was something magnificently beautiful in those quiet moments we shared.

At exactly midnight, she stood up. "Voila! Merci, Sebastian. You have no idea how grateful I am," Ana said.

"Are you finished?" I asked, anxious to see what we had accomplished together. "Can I take a look?"

"Yes and no," she said with an adorable smirk on her face. "I am finished, but you may not peek tonight. I need a few more days to add the finishing touches," she said, then hurriedly sneaked her canvas to her room.

A short while later, I stepped into a bathtub of clear, clean water, and all the newspapers were picked up and disposed of. Once my body and her living space were cleaned up, we made love patiently for the whole night.

I took nearly six baths and three days before I felt I'd really removed every crimson stain from my body and hair, but my reward was when Ana showed me her work four nights after she painted it. It was utterly fascinating to me. Somehow, she'd pulled what looked like dozens of shades of red into her work. There was so much depth and passion in it. Despite the absence of my facial features in the painting, I felt myself in it. I recalled every minute of my time on that chair, and the result was a masterpiece. *If I could go back in time,* I thought, looking at her miraculous painting, *I'd do it all over again, a thousand times.*

After that, Ana approached many Paris galleries, but luck was not on her side. All of us who knew her encouraged and supported her, and we spread the word about her everywhere we could. Antoine and Émilie told everyone they knew about her, and so did everyone else who had seen her work. Paris was full of artists, though, a known Mecca for art believers and the place where many of the greats began or eventually found themselves. To really make a success of it, artists in Paris had to really stand out.

Even the new galleries that opened preferred to work with well-known artists and rarely gave newcomers a chance. Some artists ventured there for a few months, till all their money ran out and they had nothing to carry back to their hometowns but their shattered dreams. The brave ones stayed a little longer, longing for a lucky break. Some never left Paris and chose to work odd jobs to keep themselves afloat while they continued peddling their art wherever they could, even if it meant living on the streets. The stress of it did get to Ana, and she was not a very patient person, but I had a feeling it would only be a matter of time before she found her way.

After a few months, an advertisement appeared in the newspaper Antoine worked for. Musee d'orsay would hold a two-day exhibition a month later, focusing on inspiring female artists. The tickets were priced at only five francs for spectators, and the museum would take only 25 percent of any sales; the profits from the event would be donated to a charity that supported World War II widows, a respectable initiative, since many were still struggling even decades after losing their loved ones.

Ana applied for the exhibition and heard back a week later; she would exhibit, along with five other artists. Each artist was given a wall to present their work, and Ana chose seven of her favorite paintings. When I asked why the portrait of me was not among them, she answered, "That painting did not talk to me. This is just...not the time for it," she said.

Instinct, I thought, and I could never argue with that.

Two of her works were medium sized, just thirty-six by twenty-eight inches. The remaining five were smaller, twenty-eight by sixteen, a series of sunsets. All of the paintings, though, contained her trademark reds.

The museum was simple in design, and the exhibition was not big and fancy, but over 300 people attended within the first 3 hours. That was due, in part, to the amazing publicity by the organizers, the media, and even Antoine, who played a role in exposing the word in his paper. I also made sure everyone at our museum knew about it, and Émilie told all of her art-loving friends.

Each artist stood near his or her wall as people walked by and admired the works. Some asked questions, and the artists were happy to explain. The first day, Ana really stood out, practically glowing in her white overalls, black shoes, and with a red ribbon in her hair, a simple but elegant choice. She was also the most talkative of all the artists. The second day, she was noticeably quieter, as if she was disappointed with the show. She had sold only two of her paintings from the sunset series, to an old woman who lived just outside Paris. The old lady paid 1,400 francs for both. Other than that, she only engaged in chitchat with a few people, as well as some journalists who stopped by to take some photos from time to time.

Just an hour before the end of the exhibition, a man in his mid-forties approached. He was wearing a long, brown coat over his black suit. He peered at Ana's paintings from behind his big, black glasses, then turned to her and asked, "Ana, the painter, I presume?"

"Yes, hi. I'm Ana, and this is my friend, Sebastian," she replied.

"Hello, Ana and Sebastian. I am Frank Schull," he said, presenting his card to Ana.

"You are from Miami?" she questioned, leaning over to show the card to me.

"Yes. We own several galleries in the States, but our main office is in Florida." He hesitated and looked at her paintings once more. "Interesting. Quite impressive really," he observed. "Why red, though, if I may ask."

"We are all red on the inside, are we not? Why not reflect that on the outside?" Ana replied.

"Would you accept $2,000 for the larger painting on the right, Ana, as well as the last smaller one on the right? I believe that would be about 8,700 francs."

It was evident in Ana's eyes that she was thrilled at the offer, as well as flattered by it, but she paused a moment, as if she had to think about it. "Hmm," she said. "Yes, yes, of course!" she squealed, her eyes dancing, betraying her excitement.

"It's a deal then," said Frank. "Just call the number on the card on Monday. Ask for Cindy, our secretary, and she will inform you how to ship them. Just remember the time difference. I think we are four hours behind you in Miami. By the way, do you have a phone number where I can reach you?" the American politely asked.

"Oh, how clumsy of me," she replied, a bit embarrassed. "Here is my card."

He glanced down at the white business card with the red lettering and smiled. "Great. You've done great work here, Ana. Expect a call from us soon. Well done." Then, after a shake of our hands, he walked away.

Ana looked at me, smiling from ear to ear. "I am so happy, Sebastian. We simply must celebrate. We can drink, dance, jump in the Seine...anything! Just take me out of here."

Thankfully, neither of us jumped into anything, but by the end of the night, we had decided to crash at Antoine's and Émilie's place. We were all drunk, and they insisted, since the bar was only a block away from their place. I was most thankful for it, because I didn't want my mother to see me like that.

Three weeks later, Ana visited me at The Louvre. She was still wearing a smile, but her eyes were full of tears, and she pulled me into a hug as soon as she saw me. "Oh, Sebastian, you'll never guess. I've been offered an exhibition!" she said.

"That's wonderful," I whispered in her ear. "I'm proud of you. Where?"

"Well...Miami," she answered. "Frank called an hour ago. I will accompany one other artist, a young Mexican who loves drawing in green, a real compliment for yours truly, red Ana. Frank says everybody in the States is going crazy over my work."

"When?" I asked.

"In May, just two months from now. They pay $2,000 up front, and can keep 40 percent of any sales. Frank said they will book me lodging for two weeks, the week before the show and the week after. They will even pay for my airline tickets. Of course I asked for two tickets and..." She stopped temporarily, to catch her breath, and looked at me.

"Wait. Two tickets? Why?" I asked, confused.

"You know why, Sebastian. I need you with me, at least this one last time. If all goes well there, I am not coming back though," she said, and the dam of tears released salty droplets to roll down her cheeks.

"I-I know, Ana," I stuttered. "I guess I've always known. Stop crying now. This is good news, the best news. We have two months left to do everything we've ever wanted. Let's just enjoy it," I said.

She hugged me again, harder this time. "Well, I'll be pretty busy. Frank said I should have at least fifteen paintings ready. They will shortlist ten from them. I need to work on three or four more. Perhaps, dear Sebastian, you could—"

"Only in your dreams, Ana," I said. "I don't relish the thought of being dipped in paint again, ever," I said with a grin.

"Just joking, dear. Having sex once with a red man is more than enough for a lifetime," she teased.

On May 12, a beautiful, sunny day, we arrived at the Miami airport. Our last two lovely months in Paris were rainy weeks, but summer had definitely made its way to the Sunshine State.

The days before our departure to the United States would not soon be forgotten, for they were full of precious memories. We traveled a lot and enjoyed jumping from one winery to the other in Porto during our small getaway in Portugal. We enjoyed a lot of hiking, taking in the beautiful scenery near Salzburg in

Austria. We spent many sleepless nights in Paris, the City of Lights, and we loved tasting the cuisine and drinks wherever we wandered. Our relationship had a crazy start, and we agreed that our farewell would be just as crazy as our early beginnings.

In Florida, Frank and Cindy welcomed us at the airport and gave us a ride to the apartment that would serve as Ana's temporary home for the next two weeks. I would stay only for a week, till the show was over, as I didn't want to leave my mother alone for too long. Mom didn't seem to have a problem with it, but I had never been away from her for more than a week at a time.

The apartment was situated in a nice complex that contained about fifteen flats. When we arrived, there were a few people enjoying the sun, relaxing by the big pool in the middle. The gardens were gorgeous, filled with the palm trees that were so popular all over Miami. Her apartment was on the upper floor, a two-bedroom that was far more spacious than what we were used to in Paris. The kitchen opened into a living room that could easily seat several visitors. The bedrooms were furnished with queen-sized beds and built-in wardrobes. Everything was simple but efficient, and she had all the amenities she needed there, including a large TV that picked up several American cable channels. The refrigerator was chockfull of fruits, vegetables, juice, and cheese, along with a few packs of beer. Everything was convenient and arranged well, prepared in advance for her to have a comfortable stay.

"Someone will pick you up tomorrow around noon," Frank said, "and you'll join some of the gallery staff for lunch at a restaurant on the beach. You'll love the fresh seafood there."

"Then," Cindy elaborated, "one of the staff members will take you shopping. You'll have dinner with some other art industry moguls after that."

We were informed that over the next two days, Ana would be interviewed by journalists from a few local papers, as well as a reporter from the art magazine that would cover the exhibition. Then, the preparations at the gallery would get underway.

"Hey, do you two like pizza?" Frank asked.

"Yes, of course," we answered together.

"In that case, what time would you like them to be delivered? I'm assuming you'd like to relax for the rest of today, maybe take a dip in the pool to ease off some of the jetlag."

It was all very thoughtful of him, and he was right, for as soon as they left, we hopped into our swimwear and spent hours sunbathing and frolicking around in the pool like a couple of little kids.

The next few days went according to plan. Ana flourished in her interviews; she was like a bird flying to heights she'd never been to before. Everyone was impressed, and I couldn't blame them, for she was a natural.

During one of the meetings with Frank and the gallery staff, they showed us the ten paintings they had selected. Mine was among them, but I felt they had not chosen Ana's best, a painting of a man's palm breaking through a thick cloud. I didn't say a word in front of them, but when we went back, I told Ana to insist that they include that particular piece of work in the collection. "Maybe they know more about the taste of the visitors or the critiques here, but you have fight them on this, Ana. It shows...character. You must insist," I said.

A day before the show, we all met at the gallery. It was a large, white space, with high ceilings filled with spotlights to illuminate the paintings. We were told that a few tall, black tables would be placed sporadically throughout, to create a simple, easy layout, quite like the one Musee d'orsay provided during the charity event. The minimalist approach put all the focus on the paintings themselves, which was precisely the way an art exhibition was supposed to be.

Juan Pedro, the Mexican artist, was not that young after all. In fact, he was in his late forties, and he looked a lot older, thanks to his long, gray hair. His green eyes were bright, though, and he had a good physique for a man his age. He explained that he'd been painting in the streets of Mexico City for decades. One day, an American tourist asked to take some photos of his artwork, and that was that. His work was strange, an odd mix of cubism, in abstract style, but green was his color, and he mastered in it. Juan was very excited to be showing his work for the very first time in a gallery.

The person in charge of the gallery explained the program to us briefly, including the schedule, positioning and layout, and all the details. Juan Pedro was assigned to the left side of the room, while Ana's reds would inhabit the right. He then privately discussed painting prices with Ana and Juan.

"Three of the bigger paintings will be presented at $2,500 each," Ana delightedly whispered to me, "and the remaining seven smaller ones will be priced at $1,500. Can you believe that?"

The selected paintings were delivered, and the display was set up. Ana allowed me to help choose where to put the paintings, because she felt my years at The Louvre gave me more insight and experience than most of those present. I was happy when no one objected, but I did have some objections of my own.

"Ana, it is truly a pity that *The Palm* is not here," I reiterated.

She did not reply.

"Also, Juan Pedro should charge the most for that little painting over there. It is, by far, his best work."

She nodded but still didn't say a word.

Around four p.m., we finished and headed back to the apartment. The next day would certainly be an emotional day for Ana. Little did I know, however, that it would be just as emotional for me.

At six p.m., the phone rang. "Sebastian, it's your mother," said Madam Claudia, Mom's friend. "She… Sebastian, she has had a stroke. I'm sorry to tell you this, but she is in the hospital, in a coma. I found her lying there unconscious when I came to get her so we could go to the theater with Madam Susanne. We managed to call an ambulance in time," she said, then went on to fill me in on the rest of the details.

Ana was as shocked as I was when I told her. We called Frank, and rushed over right away. Ana did her best to comfort me, and she even asked Frank if she had to be there during her exhibition.

"No, Ana," I interrupted. "I won't even let you think about that. This is important to you, and you cannot miss it…for anything."

The earliest flight was nine in the morning, and Frank quickly booked it for me. I hated that I had to leave Ana, and she hated that she could not be there for me in a difficult time. The greatest thing about our time together is that we understood each other well, and neither of us had hard feelings about it.

The night we got the news, neither of us could sleep for many hours. The next morning, when she had finally stopped tossing and turning, I could not bear to wake her. I just looked at her sleeping, blew her a kiss, then made my way down to the waiting taxi. In a blur, I was at the airport, and later that very same day, I was back in Paris, without Ana by my side.

Chapter Three

The plane arrived on time, but the airport was very busy and crowded. The line for the taxi was disastrous; there must have been at least fifty people in front of me. I had to wait at least an hour, and it was the longest hour of my life because I was on fire, so desperate to reach my ailing mother. When I saw an old man who was third in line, I dragged my luggage over to him and explained that my mother was ill. Lucky for me, he was heading in the same direction, and he was a very kind man who insisted we share the ride. The taxi dropped me off at the hospital first, and I thanked my fellow commuter, then ran inside.

As soon as I reached the intensive care unit, I was greeted by Madam Claudia and Madam Susanne. It had been exactly twenty-one hours since my mother was found unconscious in the living room, already dressed for a night out with her friends. Doctors estimated that the stroke had happened just less than an hour before she was found.

"She is responsive, they say, but they haven't let us in to see her," said Madam Susanne, crying.

"Responsive? That's good," I said, relieved. "Where is the doctor now?"

"I just saw him go in Room 23," Madam Claudia replied.

All three of us hurried to the room and knocked twice before the door opened.

Dr. Pierre was the head neurologist at the hospital, the man in charge of treating my mother. He was in his early fifties and was about my height, almost completely bald, save a sparse bit of hair on the sides of his head. All his features were small, and his black eyes reminded me of coat buttons. In spite of that, though, when he spoke, he was like a giant; his heavy, booming voice could be heard all the way down the long corridor. "Sebastian, I believe," the doctor asked, shaking my hand with a strong grip.

I nodded.

"Welcome back. I heard you were in the States."

"Yes, Doctor."

"Please have a seat, all of you," the doctor said. Once we sat, he continued, "Sebastian, I'm happy to report that your mother is fine now. She is responding well to treatment."

"What happened to her, Dr. Pierre?" I asked."

"Well, she suffered a brain stroke, or an ischemic stroke. A blood clot formed in one of the arteries that supplies the brain, causing an obstruction. This was treated, but there was some damage already to some of her brain cells. Your mother is lucky she was found so quickly after her stroke. Otherwise, it would have likely been fatal," Dr. Pierre said, looking each of us in the eye one by one.

"Damage to her brain cells? What do you mean? I-I don't understand," I said.

"Her vision is good, and her memory is perfect. She even asked about you and mentioned you were in Miami. Her speech is somewhat slurred, but that will improve with time. Her problem is on the right side, and we've had no response at all in her right leg. She's experiencing some numbness in her right arm, though, and that's a good sign. We need to keep her for at least a week, and then we have to lay out a long-term treatment plan. All is good Sebastian. Your mother is lucky, as this could have been much, much worse. Since she is awake now, you may see her, but only for a few minutes," the doctor concluded.

"Can we see her together?" Madam Claudia asked, pointing to her friend beside her.

The doctor nodded. "Sure," he said with a smile.

I gained all the strength in the world in that moment, just enough to utter three words: "Thank you, Doctor."

My mother was in a smaller room by herself, at the very end of the hall in the ICU. As soon as I walked in and she saw me, some of the color returned to her face.

"Sebastian! You're here!" she said excitedly.

I hurried over to hug her. "Mother, how are you?"

"It was so strange. I just felt a little headache coming on, and then I couldn't see well. I don't know what happened after that," she answered.

"It's all right. You're going to be fine, Mother, and you'll be back home in no time. Dr. Pierre just wants to run some tests for a few days."

"How was the show? Miami? Ana?" she asked.

"All good. All is good, Mother," I said, as I truly felt it was, even if I wasn't sure what happened in Miami after I left. "Madam Susanne and Madam Claudia are here. They want to see you, but then you have to rest. You must do everything the doctors and nurses tell you, Mother. I'll stay over at the hospital tonight, so you won't be alone," I said, then gave her a gentle kiss and left the room.

I talked with the nurse and told her I would be back in a few hours, as I had to go home and change clothes after my long trip. "If anything happens or she needs anything, just call me at this number," I said, handing her a slip of paper with my home phone on it.

A minute after I walked in my door, the phone rang.

"Sebastian!" Ana said as soon as I picked up the phone, almost before I could even say hello. "I've been so worried. I tried your place a dozen times," she said loudly over the loud noises in the background. "Tell me your mother is all right."

"She is doing fine now. She had a brain stroke. The doctor said she might not be able to walk alone again. Her right leg is nonresponsive. Still, things could have gone much worse. She'll get through it, Ana. She is a strong woman. She always has been."

"I wish I was there with you, but—"

"I know, Ana. Tell me about your exhibition. How are things?" I cut in.

"There are still a few hours to go, but it's been amazing so far. Can you believe I sold everything?" she said.

"I can believe it, and I'm not surprised. I've always believed in you and your work. Who ended up having to enjoy my red butt on a daily basis?"

"A fortunate old couple. I believe your majesty will spice up their life."

"Ana!" a voice cried from somewhere behind her.

"I have to go now," she said. "I'll call you later this week, once things calm down. Oh, but before I go, I wanted to mention that *The Palm* was the showstopper."

"The Palm? They displayed it?" I asked.

"Yes, because I said so, like you told me to. Frank obliged, and the response justified my request. You've always had a great eye for art, Sebastian. I can't thank you enough for the support. Juan Pedro also told me to thank you. He sold his small painting for a price higher than the rest. You were spot on."

With a smile on my face for Ana's and Juan Pedro's good fortune, I hung up the phone and walked into the bathroom. Just as I was drawing a warm bath for myself, the phone rang again.

"We found out about an hour ago," Antoine said. "Ana called, and... Well, anyway, how is she now?"

"Mom is recovering. I'm only home for a bit, long enough to take a bath and a quick nap. You think you two could come over in about two hours and give me a ride to the hospital? We can talk more on the way."

As soon as my head touched the pillow, I slept like a baby. A couple hours later, my friends picked me up and escorted me to the hospital. I spent that night by my mother's side and the remaining week as well.

A week later, we were back home, and changes needed to be made in the house to accommodate my mother's new situation. Our entire lifestyle had to change, and it was going to take a lot of getting used to for both of us. Life, aging, and sickness were a harsh reality, and now we had to face that and adapt to it the best we could.

Before we left the hospital, Dr. Pierre explained in detail what the causes of the stroke might have been. He also discussed the actions we should follow to prevent a recurrence in the future. My mother was closing in on 70 and was a heavy smoker. We didn't realize it, but she'd been suffering from high blood pressure for quite a while. Now, she had to give up smoking, as well as red meat. She was instructed to eat plenty of fish, chicken, and vegetables instead, grilled or boiled and no frying. Dr. Pierre also noted that her sugar levels were borderline dangerous. She could enjoy no more sweets, other than a little fruit from time to time. Alcohol wasn't advised, though a glass of wine every once in a while was fine.

On top of that, she needed some special care. Her right arm felt heavy and numb, though the limb's response to heat and pressure had improved a bit during her week in the hospital. She could even move her little finger slightly. Dr. Pierre was optimistic about her arm, but there was little hope for any recovery in her leg.

Mother had to visit the hospital three times a week for the first two months for physiotherapy. They worked on inducing blood flow to the area to strengthen the muscles and regenerate the damaged nerves. As time passed, depending on her response, the treatment would change.

Catherin came from South Africa and offered to stay for a month. Together, we made the adjustments to what was needed. I met with an engineer to redesign our home and with the contractor who would carry out his instructions. One of the walls of my mother's bedroom had to go, so the room would open directly to one of the bathrooms, making it easier for her to move about the flat. Support points were installed all around the place, and furniture was moved a bit to allow space for her wheelchair. We used two big boards to create a ramp for the stairs whenever she had to go out.

Catherin bought one of the best available wheelchairs, a manual one produced by Meyra, a German company. After consulting with Dr. Pierre, a type with a flip back and removable armrests was chosen; it would ease her transfer in and out of the chair. It also had removable footrests so my mother could propel herself with her working foot during recovery.

Dr. Pierre explained that good posture, even in the wheelchair, was essential after Mom's stroke. He also addressed the importance of proper cleaning and taught us all about the best caregiving to help her avoid the worst enemy of any paralyzed patient, the development of ulcers.

During the first month, my sister and I took care of our mother, but since we eventually had to get back to our normal lives, we hired a specialized caregiver. Mrs.

André was in her forties, and in spite of her small size, she was rather physically strong and could carry a lot on her broad shoulders. Of course, her services did not come cheap; it cost more than I made at the museum. She worked five days a week, from eight till five, when I returned from work to take over. Mrs. André took Mother to the hospital for her therapy sessions, took care of all her necessities, and cooked meals for her.

It put a smile on my mother's face when Madam Claudia and Madam Susanne stopped by several times a week as well. They had all learned a lesson and had quit smoking, but they loved talking and knitting and didn't seem to miss those fancy, handcrafted cigarettes boxes.

Little by little, my mother showed more progress in her arm. She could move her fingers slowly, but that was not enough for her. Frustration and impatience began to get the best of her, and her mood became less tolerable. Six months after her stroke, she did not feel anything had improved enough.

I met with Dr. Pierre and explained the situation to him, but he assured me she was receiving the best care the hospital had to offer. "There is a new clinic in Marne, opened about a year ago. It's about three hours from here, and it offers Chinese treatments. I've heard about good results from my colleagues, but the treatment is rather expensive," he said.

A week later, my mother and I went to that clinic that was situated in a beautiful house that overlooked Lake Der-Chantecoq, one of the largest manmade reservoirs in Europe. It was formed to hold the water of the River Marne to prevent flooding of the Seine in Paris.

A French doctor of Chinese origin, Yang, was the man who established the clinic. He was an orthopedic who had graduated from Peking Union Medical College Hospital in China, one of the most reputed universities in all of Asia. The doctor was in his sixties and had been working in traditional Chinese medicine for over four decades. He ventured into Paris ten years prior and started a small clinic near Champagne. When his business grew, he purchased five acres of land to build his new clinic. The mansion was beautiful and white, with an Asian-style, ornate façade. The roof, however, was covered with red tile, just like the rooftops of the houses in the Mediterranean. There were ten patient rooms, all of them fitted with floor-to-ceiling windows that overlooked the gorgeous lake. There were also four small treatment rooms with floors of blue, glossy marble tiles and pearly white walls. There were many Asian statues and artistic fountains scattered around the gardens, along with flowers of every imaginable color and several small mandarin trees.

It was said that Dr. Yang's family owned vast agricultural lands back in China. He came from a wealthy line, and he and his brother inherited it all. He did not share his brother's interest in farming, as he was more into medicine and the use of herbs, so he eventually sold his share to his brother. Then, after years of practice back home, the good doctor decided to move abroad.

Dr. Yang's therapy included applying an herbal mixture to affected areas for a time, followed by sessions of acupuncture. The thin, single-use needles triggered specific nervous areas, inducing blood flow. That was followed by intermittent periods of massage with herbal extracts. The treatment also included normal physical therapy and extensive exercise.

I drove my mother there every Friday night around eight and picked her up at five p.m. on the following Sundays. I spent those nights in a hotel close by. It was a kind of a retreat for me, a bit of a reprieve from the hustle of the city. I spent time reading more about the world of art, the latest news about museum acquisitions around the globe, and stories about new and emerging artists.

As the weeks passed by, my mother improved. I wasn't sure if it was because of the treatment at the clinic, her regular weekly therapy in Paris with Dr. Pierre, or just a better psychological perspective, but I was happy about it. Something was working, and as long as things were getting better, no one complained, and we continued with Dr. Yang's treatment.

Three months later, Mother's arm was mobile. It was still heavy, but she could move all her fingers and her hand normally. Her leg still responded to nothing, and we had to accept the fact that she would have to live without the use of it. Our time at the clinic was over, and we were content with everything except the small fortune we'd spent. Most of my mother's savings were wiped out, and I barely had anything left over from my wages at the museum. Catherin tried to pitch in, but her husband's business wasn't going well, and they had a lot on their plate with a growing family of five.

My job seemed to be moving at a slower pace. As technology advanced, we had less to do with authentication and preservation as we had in the past. My interest was also not quite as piqued as it was during my first thorough years. Every now and then, I had second thoughts, but it was still my job, so I continued to ride my bicycle to the museum as soon as Mrs. André arrived. I did, however, return home earlier and earlier every evening.

I had a chance to talk to Ana sometimes. She told me she was doing well, traveling all over North America. She had a demanding schedule, taking part in galleries from San Francisco to Toronto, Quebec to Boston. She was nicknamed Ana Rouge, Red Ana. Some newspapers had even dubbed her the Red Queen. Her work was flourishing, but I could tell from her voice that she was exhausted.

"I wish I could come to Paris soon," she said one night. "I wish I could see you, hear you play your guitar. Antoine, Émilie... I miss you all. I want to get away from all this."

"The flow is with you now, Ana. Don't slow down. Time waits for no one."

"I guess you're right," she said after a sigh. "You know, there are hundreds of artists here who do great work, yet they have nowhere but the streets to show them off. I know how lucky I am, Sebastian. Also, to be honest, the money's really good. Anyway, I still want to come visit you all for a little while," she finished before we said our goodbyes.

I couldn't say the same about my finances, as my mother's medical condition has taken its toll on us. We were spending more than what we were earning, and my savings were shrinking by the month. I had been working hard for the past seven years, and all I had to show for it was a mere 40,000 francs to my name. I used to save nearly half of that each year, but for the past year or so, my savings had been dwindling.

Fortunately, I had no rent to pay, because my grandfather had left the flat to us. Nevertheless, I knew we had to be more cautious with our spending. We started to cut down on our weekly groceries and canceled our newspaper subscription. I even got rid of my library card; if it wasn't for Monsieur Daniel passing away a week earlier and his children closing down his beautiful library for good, I would have never bought those twenty books lying in front of me. I simply couldn't resist the offer of one franc per book. It was a pity to see that place close, an icon in our area that used to occupy a corner between two streets. There were so many memories there. I could still recall Grandfather purchasing books for me there when I was a child, and I loved getting lost in those halls. Now, with the books all gone, it was just an empty white space, listed for rent.

"That's life," my mother said sadly as she sat in her wheelchair and passed books to me. She cried a lot that night. I heard her but felt it was best to let her blow her steam.

Despite getting better and despite her friends being around to try to cheer her, my mother harbored a deep sadness. She needed to feel more important. After all, in the past, not even the Nazis could stop her from working. She felt useless after her stroke, and that destroyed her. I couldn't bear to hear her crying, and I couldn't stop thinking about her sobs.

The next day, we were told that the museum had plans to renovate the whole place, as well as to increase the size of some of the halls. In order to finance that expansion, leasing or selling some of the stocked works to other museums and galleries was the best option.

We were asked to prepare an updated list of all the stored valuables, indicating their condition and any related information. We had a month to prepare the list for presentation, but we worked hard at it and managed to offer those reports a week before the deadline.

Management decided that over 1,000 pieces would be sold or leased over a scheduled period of time. All of them were placed in one large room, and potentials buyers visited once a week to look at them. Our museum would only sell or lease to reputed museums or galleries that were held in the highest regard.

Week after week, the stockpile shrank. I was sad to see so many lovely pieces go, and I felt envious of the buyers. *I wish I could take those pieces home myself,* I thought more than once.

One day, three men visited from London, from Pearce Gallery. They had been in the art and antiquities business for about twenty years. It was said that they had an expensive lot of paintings and sculptures, including masterpieces by Van Gogh, Renoir, Degas, Rodin, and others. Their collections were leased to museums around the world for good money. From the minute they entered, we could tell they were renowned traders. They had a certain swagger about them, in the way they talked and sauntered about the place in their black suits and shiny shoes, carrying their black, leather bags. Each of the sharp men had a folder in his hand with a list of what was still on offer by our museum. They were very organized and knew exactly what they wanted. The trio was interested in only what was for sale, not anything for lease or rent.

The oldest of the three, Matthew Pearce, was around 40 years old. He asked about the paintings, as that was the line he worked in. The other two men were about my age, in their late twenties or early thirties. They examined the list of sculptures and furniture, as well as old artifacts. They whispered things in Matthew's ear and listened to his replies but never uttered one word to us. Matthew did all the talking, in a most arrogant way, refusing to make eye contact. Several times during the visit, he pointed at me and asked me questions, without making any effort to step closer to me. They were there for over an hour and selected twenty pieces altogether, but Matthew had chosen only two of them. The selected ones were put aside, and Matthew said a few words to one of his men as he was walking out.

Finally, one of the younger men spoke to us and informed us, "Someone from our firm will send the official request later today. We will need all these shipped by the end of the week."

After Matthew signed all the papers I presented to him, he turned to his men on the way out and snobbishly said, "What a waste of time. I am more interested in Ivan Olic's stock in Trogir on Thursday. He has some real jewels there, and the prices will be much better compared to what these people have to offer."

Trogir, Thursday, Ivan Olic, I thought, making a mental note. Then, as soon as I finished work that day, I paid my old mentor a visit to share what was cooking up in my mind.

I hadn't seen Professor Schmidt for over eight months. He had called the day after he found out about my mother's stroke, and he sweetly visited to check on us, with a large bouquet of flowers in tow. That brightened my mother's mood, and we laughed a lot that day. This time, however, it was me who would surprise him with a visit.

I reached his place around six in the evening, carrying a fine bottle of Pinot Noir wine, the kind I knew he was fond of. I knocked on his door a few times, but there was no answer.

A minute later, a cute little girl opened the neighbor's door. "Looking for Professor Schmidt?"

"Yes, as a matter of fact, I am, young lady. Do you know where I might—"

"He is at the café at the end of the street, playing chess," she replied as played with her doll that was almost as big as she was.

"Why, thank you," I said, then turned to head down the stairs.

A few minutes later, I spotted the professor in the café, busy at the chess board, just as the little girl had said.

"Sebastian, dear boy!" he said boisterously, standing as soon as he saw me. "Leaving The Louvre, aren't you?"

"Hmm? What? Who?" I asked, confused.

"Sit down for a minute. I just need four moves, and I shall defeat my old friend, then join you," he announced, looking snidely at the man beside him.

The old man nodded to me politely.

"Get us two glasses of wine, will you? I will drink that later" he said, pointing to the brown bag in my right hand.

"Will do, Professor Schmidt," I said with a grin, shaking my head as I took a seat a few tables away.

Five minutes later, he joined me.

"Now, what makes you think I am leaving?" I asked immediately.

"Well, with all the new stuff coming in, I don't suppose you're as busy as you were before. It's time you move on. So tell me, what can this old man do for you today?"

"Do you know a guy named Ivan Olic?"

"Ivan? The Croat?

"Yugoslavian," I answered.

"He prefers Croatian, but yes, I know a bit about him. I know he's a great admirer of art, a man with a good collection." Professor Schmidt paused to take a sip of the wine I'd ordered.

"Tell me more, Professor," I urged.

"Well, Ivan was born to a poor family, but he managed to build an empire out of nothing. See, his parents died in a car accident while he was just a teenager. They weren't that young, his parents. His mother had him late, in her mid-forties. Anyway, Ivan turned out to be a very intelligent engineer. After World War II, he was part of group that revolutionized the shipping industry. Later, he started his own ship-building business.

"During the past twenty years, he has been amassing a large art collection from all over. I met him twice in The Louvre, back in the sixties. I found him to be a very sophisticated gentleman, socially connected all over the world. Last I heard, he retired completely from his work and handed most of his business to his son and daughter. Why do you ask, though, Sebastian? What's Ivan got to do with you?" Professor Schmidt said as he brought his face closer to mine.

I explained to him what I found out from the gentleman who had visited the museum earlier that day. I also told him about my own financial difficulties, and I let him know that he was right, that my work was just not that inspiring anymore. "It's all machines now, and everything is outsourced. Our instinct and hard work aren't as necessary. I've been thinking about this for some time," I said. "There are hundreds of artists with nowhere to go, with no one giving them a chance. The galleries I've seen don't really require much effort to set them up, so I've been thinking of opening my own place," I said. "I even have a place in mind."

"What place?" the professor asked.

"Remember Monsieur Daniel's library, two buildings down from my place in Le Marais?"

"Certainly," he said, then took another sip of wine.

"Well, he sadly passed away, and his heirs didn't want to run the library anymore. They are looking to rent the place. They already moved all the books out," I said.

"Ah, well, that Daniel was a good man. I knew him for a long time. He was a hardworking fellow. I hope he's in a better place now. It's a really good space,

Sebastian. With a few special touches, it could be utilized well as a gallery," he agreed.

"I know it won't be easy, but I'd like to use part of it for a gallery of permanent works and part as a space for inspired artists to show off their new pieces. It will be difficult, and I will need the help of many." I paused and looked seriously at my old friend and mentor. "Professor, I know you have been retired for a few years now, enjoying your relaxed life, but I am wondering if—"

"My boy, do you think an old man likes playing chess every day forever? Of course I'd love to get back to handling art again. I am in, Sebastian. Where the hell have you been anyway?" He then sneered and crashed his cane against the floor twice, motioning to the waiter for a second glass.

I put my hand on his. "With your help, I can find art the people in Paris will love to see," I said, gesturing to the waiter to fetch me a second glass as well.

We spent another hour drinking and remembering our good times, and by the end of the night, we were both looking forward to what we hoped would be even better ones.

Back home again, I called a friend of mine at the travel agency and asked him to book me a flight on Wednesday. The earliest left Charles de Gaulle airport 6:45 a.m. I would land in Zagreb, then travel for four hours by car to Trogir. Before I hung up the phone, everything was booked.

The next day, I handed The Louvre my resignation. I was determined, and there was no looking back. They were sad to see me go, but they knew I had many responsibilities and goals of my own, and they refused to stand in my way. I also called Monsieur Daniel's daughter Isabelle to inquire about renting the place.

Wednesday morning, I landed in Zagreb, carrying a small brown bag. In it was one ironed, long-sleeved, white shirt, a floral shirt, some dark blue jeans, and my sleeping clothes. I was light on luggage but full of high hopes.

Chapter Four

I slept during most of the car ride to Trogir. I had been awake since four in the morning and could not sleep a second during the flight to Zagreb, so it was no surprise that the steady lullaby of the taxi cruising down the road had me fast asleep within minutes.

Darko, the tall, blond driver I hired at the airport woke me up fifteen minutes before we reached town. "You say Ivan Olic, no?" he asked in broken English.

"Yes. Ivan Olic," I affirmed.

"I know someone at post office, near old town. Might be able to help," Darko informed me.

We parked the car right on the shore, at the place where the town and harbor began. Trogir, on the Adriatic coast in Split-Dalmatia County, was founded by the Greeks, who first settled there in the third century BC. Its original name was Tragos, Greek for "the male goat." I could tell straightaway that the little burg was steeped in history. After it was ruled by the Greeks, it saw governorship by the Romans and, most importantly, the Venetians. Thus, there was plenty of Venetian architecture and red tiled roofs to admire throughout the city.

Darko and I walked into the old town to meet his acquaintance, and I truly hoped he had some information about the man I was searching for. It wasn't easy to keep up with the long-legged blond as he speed-walked through the narrow, cobblestone streets, past churches, statues, and stunning squares. I was very impressed with the beauty and the historical preservation of the place. *No wonder Ivan Olic loves history and art,* I thought. *This place is a painting itself.*

Signs to the post office showed we were 200m away.

"Monsieur Sebastian," Darko said when we saw a sign indicating that the post office was only twenty meters away, "you should eat small bite at café. I will go talk to my friend. I hope it is your lucky day."

In the café, I ordered black coffee and a cheese sandwich, read through the notes I'd written about Ivan Olic, and enjoyed watching the passersby. Fifteen minutes later, Darko returned, giving me the thumbs-up, and I quickly paid the bill and followed him.

"Your man Ivan is well-known figure," Darko said. "He doesn't live here in Trogir but on that small island out there." He paused to point to a place in the sea. "I have address. It will be twenty minutes across the bridge and up the hill."

We made our way back to the taxi, and a half-hour later, I found myself standing outside one of the most beautiful villas I had ever seen.

Located on one of the slopes in the hills of Čiovo Island, overlooking the beautiful town of Trogir on the other side, was a three-story Dalmatian, a Venetian-style palace.

The house was huge and occupied an enormous plot of land. We parked right outside the tall, golden gate and cast curious glances at one another before we climbed out of the car. I couldn't stop staring at the place. It was fashioned from white and gray stones, intricately carved and decorated with angels, fairies, gods, and animals all over the exterior. The oval-shaped windows stretched from floor to ceiling. The roof was colorful and stylish, with a turquoise tiled dome on one side and a red tiled pyramid on the other. Each of the three floors boasted a terrace that wrapped all the way around the house.

I rang the bell a few times and finally saw a giant of a man approaching, with a large German Shephard walking beside him. As the black man neared, I was astonished by his physical size. I thought Darko was tall, but this man dwarfed him at more than seven feet tall. He was all muscle, too, a walking tank, and his dog was almost as intimidating as he was, especially when he started barking at us. I didn't know who I was more afraid of, the big man or his aggressive pet.

He said something, but I couldn't understand a word of it.

"Francais, English?" I asked, gesturing to let him know I didn't understand.

"What do you want?" the big man demanded.

"Mr. Ivan Olic. Is he here? Can I see him?" I replied, trying to keep the tremble out of my voice.

"Do you have an appointment? You a journalist?" the giant asked, still staring into my eyes.

"No. Just... Can you give this to him and let him know I'd like to see him?" I asked, handing my card through the gate.

"Wait here, and don't move. Max gets upset easily," he said, then commanded his dog to sit and stay as he turned to make his way to the garden behind the house.

I looked at the dog and slowly moved backward, toward Darko. I thanked my driver for everything, then gave him permission to leave. "I'll take it from here," I said.

"Good luck," he wished me again, then hurried to get as far away from the dog as he could. I couldn't blame him, of course; as nice as the house was, that humongous man and his animal would have scared the hell out of anyone.

Soon, the big man returned, unlocked the gate, and welcomed me in. "Mr. Ivan is waiting for you. Come," he said.

As we walked across the garden, toward the back of the house, with that giant and that terrifying canine beside me, I felt like a child walking politely next to his strict teacher, following his exact steps. He led me through the perfectly manicured lawn, past olive, pomegranate, fig, and citrus trees and a beautiful layout of red and white flowers. Finally, we reached a terrace that overlooked the sea and the lovely town of Trogir.

In the middle of the terrace was a swimming pool made of square-cut, shining blue tiles. There was a nice bar beside it, with three stools made of white stone. At the bar, a gray-haired man with a light beard was sitting, looking over at us through his dark sunglasses and clutching his glass of an orange-colored beverage.

"Mr. Ivan?" I said, walking over to shake his hand.

"So, Sebastian, I don't recall the people at The Louvre confirming my invitation to the auction tomorrow. Correct me if I am wrong," he said, still holding my card in his hand.

"With all due respect, Mr. Ivan, I am not here on behalf of The Louvre," I replied.

"You're not?" Ivan asked, lifting his shades to reveal light blue eyes, surrounded by a few wrinkles. Without the glasses, it was also easier to determine his real age, as his crows' feet made it clear that he was in his mid-sixties.

"I am here for myself and no one else. As a matter of fact, I resigned from The Louvre a few days ago," I said.

"If you do not mind my asking, how old are you, Sebastian?"

"I am 30, sir."

"You resigned from The Louvre at just 30 years old? Hmm. Brave man." He paused to take a sip of his drink, then continued, "Beautiful weather today, wouldn't you agree? Do you have any swimwear in your little bag?"

"No, I—"

"No worries," he interrupted, then pointed at the giant. "Idris, please get this young man something to wear."

The man nodded, then went to do as he was told, taking Max with him.

"What would you like to drink?" Ivan asked.

"I'll have whatever you're having. It looks refreshing," I answered.

"It is," he said. "It's a mix of vodka, red grapefruit, lemon, and a bit of salt. You'll love it."

"Salt?" I questioned, then shrugged. "Why not?"

Idris was back in short order, carrying some black shorts, and I was thankful he'd left the dog behind.

"There is a changing room right behind the open kitchen. Have a quick shower and put those shorts on," Ivan said. "Then you can explain to me why a 30-year-old Parisian flew all the way to my place a day before an auction I will be holding," he said before diving into the pool.

For the next hour, I filled Mr. Ivan in on all there was to know about me. We discussed my upbringing, my education, my family, my time at The Louvre, my love of art, and, most importantly, the difficulty of my mother's condition and how it affected her mentally and all of us financially.

"I want to open a place of my own. My mother can help manage it. She used to run a company with her father, even when Nazis tried to overrun the place every week," I explained. "I am thinking of splitting the place into a permanent gallery and a temporary one. With my passion for art and with all I've learned about it over the years, I'm sure I will be successful. I've observed so many wonderful and talented unknown artists all over Paris, and I want to give them a chance to expose their work. I just need some nice pieces for my permanent collection to help my gallery stand out, so I can attract true art lovers."

"And why has that brought you here?" Ivan asked.

"Well, I came here, sir, to see if you have any pieces available at a good price, before the auction tomorrow. I don't know if it's possible on short notice, but I had to come here to try."

"Of course it's possible," Ivan said, then winked at me. "I own everything that is to be up for bid, and it is a private auction, by invitation only. Only thirty people will be in attendance, a few private collectors, as well as some representing different firms and museums. I suppose there will be thirty-one, including you!" He smiled, then splashed a bit with his feet. "You know, I really love my pool. I've made so many business deals right here, though this might be the last. Let's go inside, Sebastian, and I'll give you a preview of what will be up for grabs tomorrow. They were planning to pick it up in a few hours. You got here just in time."

Ivan took me inside to show me the 121 items he planned to auction off, now housed in a big space that used to be a dining room. The room was a museum all its own, and I felt as if I'd stepped into heaven. The three crystal chandeliers hanging above us must have weighed half a ton each, and the light from them reflected off the sparkling granite floors, making the mini-gallery all the more majestic.

"Mr. Ivan, just so we're clear, I only have $15,000 from my savings and the sale of a gold watch I inherited from my grandfather. I can spare only $10,000. I hope I am not wasting your time," I said as I put on a pair of gloves Ivan had passed to me.

"First, you must forget the mister and call me just Ivan. Second, I didn't ask how much you've got to spare. Now, let me show you around."

I smiled sheepishly and followed him.

"This lot of three Chinese porcelain vases from the Jiajing period of the Ming dynasty, sixteenth century, were of imperial use. They will go first," he said, lifting the vases for me to see.

With his permission, I carefully took the vases to look them over. They were red and white, with dragon and sea designs, and they were all in mint condition. "So well preserved, Mr....er, Ivan," I replied, correcting myself instantly.

"Do you see those ten swords? Those four are Ottoman. I am sure you have seen them at your museum. The other six are from the first crusade, eleventh century."

"A lovely stock," I replied.

"Here, we have a Bornholm clock, built in 1749, one of the best grandfather clocks ever made, in my opinion.

Look at that wood! It is still working, with amazing precision for its age," he elaborated.

"I have to admit that the Danish are excellent clockmakers," I said.

Impressed with my knowledge, Ivan continued, "Those four rugs are from Isfahan, sixteenth century. The colors and designs are amazing, but feel them. Have you ever touched anything softer?"

"Never," I answered, running my hands across the surface of one of the rugs.

Ivan then pulled a magnifying glass out of a drawer before speaking about his next treasures. "This is a Quran, tenth century, written by hand in Kufic calligraphy, as well as a Bible in Latin from Spain, around the ninth century, and a Torah from the twelfth century. We also have several maps drawn by Ibn Battuta, the Islamic scholar in the fourteenth century, along with dozens of other scrolls containing historically significant treaties and royal pardons. I even have a one-page letter by your French compatriot Victor Hugo to his dear friend Paul Meurice. I am—"

"Victor Hugo?" I cut in, then took the magnifying glass from him and held it in front of the framed letter. "My grandfather met him, said he bumped into Mr. Hugo while he was a child. If he only knew what I'm holding in my hand right now!"

"Bumped into him?" Ivan shook his head and chuckled. "In that case, take it. It's yours, a gift from me. Just don't say a word," he said before he walked over to the right side of the room, to a large table covered with cloth.

Oh, Grandpa! You wouldn't believe this! I thought, jumping with excitement inside myself as I grinned down at the letter.

Ivan removed the cloth to expose five sculptures of various sizes.

"Hmm. Rodin and Alberto Giacometti. Impressive, Ivan. Very impressive pieces indeed," I said, still beaming.

"Yes, I suppose there will be a bidding war over them tomorrow," he said proudly, then let out a booming laugh that rocked the whole room. "Finally, let me show you some paintings and drawings, the things you came all this way to see. See those twenty framed miniatures on the right wall?"

I nodded.

"I will sell those in four lots, five paintings each. Here are two from Jan von Eyck, and this small but beautiful mythological scene is by Peter Paul Rubens. There are other works of Jan van Dornicke from the sixteenth century and Horenbout, from the sixteenth century as well."

Looking at those beauties in front of me, I felt like I was back in The Louvre again. The man knew real art, and I was privileged to see it.

Ivan put his hand on my shoulder. "You mentioned that you have $10,000 to spend. I suppose with that amount, you could purchase one of those lots, though not that one with Rubens. Consider it yours though. Sebastian, you must have the best lot for your money, because you came all this way to visit me."

As I shook the man's hand, I was floating in the seventh sky, too thankful to even speak.

"You're welcome," he said, sensing my great gratitude by the look on my face. "Now, let me show you my last five pieces for sale."

We walked through a door on the left and were suddenly standing in his library. It was a very simple but cozy room, home to a brown leather armchair, a round, brown oak table with a globe on top, a golden table lamp next to it, and shelves that seemed sad to be so empty. On the wall, though, were his five paintings.

"Sorry the room seems dull. No books here. I donated them all to our national library a week ago. The paintings are the real gems here. Come closer. They won't bite," he coaxed when he saw me staring at them. "You have been living with the likes of them for years at The Louvre," Ivan said, standing next to the treasures.

"I just... I learned from my teacher at The Louvre to always admire art from afar first, to gain a first impression," I said, remembering the professor's wise words.

"Your teacher? You mean Schmidt, don't you?" Ivan inquired.

"Yes, before he retired a few years back," I replied, walking slowly toward the artwork.

"Retired? From The Louvre, maybe, but never fully. That man will work till his last breath on his dying day," he said.

"True, and I'm glad for it," I replied. "I need him."

"It is good to be in his company," Ivan said.

"So, there is Renoir on the left, late 1800s. Magical. Below that, in those lovely beaming colors, that nice fruit basket, is Henri Matisse. Morocco would be my guess, sometime after 1912."

Ivan nodded. "Go on, my boy."

Pleased that my art knowledge was pleasing to the collector, I went on, "As for that piece on the right... Hmm. Wait. Don't tell me."

"French, pre-cubist," Ivan hinted.

"Jean Metzinger? Yes, Jean," I said, a bit loudly and quite proud of myself.

"Correct!" he said, clapping his hands together.

"Below that is definitely Gauguin, Tahiti influence."

"Now, what about the bigger one? Venetian," Ivan said, pointing at the one in the middle.

"It is fascinating. Ah, the Italian renaissance. I just want to really look at it closely," I said.

"Take as long as you like to enjoy all of them. I will meet you outside," Ivan said, then walked out of the room.

The painting depicted some kind of a scene from the Armageddon, with angels, the divinity, devils, blood, thunder, and fire. It was a masterpiece from Titian. "The great Italian Tiziano Vecelli. What a beauty. It's just...poetry, life," I muttered to myself before I walked out to find Ivan.

"Well?" he said when he saw me.

"How?" I said.

"Excuse me?"

"How can you give all this up? Why?" I asked.

"Sebastian, all these paintings and pieces are alive, just like you and me. They deserve care, attention, emotions. They must be shown off, felt, appreciated. Don't you agree?" he asked, looking me directly in the eyes.

I looked around the room once again and nodded, approving of his every word.

"I have enjoyed them for the past twenty or thirty years. I have cried with them, talked to them, lived with them, and shown them off. Now, I can no longer do that. Gone are the days when I could invite people from all over to showcase their beauty. I spent hours explaining the essence behind each piece. Art must be shared with the world, and I am not the man to do that anymore. Come outside with me," he said as we left the museum of a room.

Outside on the terrace that overlooked Trogir and the sea, Ivan pointed. "See that land far to the left, next to that big ship with the checkered black and yellow flag?"

"Yes. That is a large plot of land," I observed.

"I have the approval of the municipality, as well as their blessing. I want to do something remarkable for this community. I have tried to help in decades past, but I do not feel I've done enough. I am growing old, Sebastian, approaching 70 in no time. As they say, it's now or never. There is so much more I can do for the people here."

"For what?" I asked, confused.

"I even bought a small house nearby, so I can keep an eye on the daily developments. I'm going to sell this place. I will probably take in several millions tomorrow from the sale, and it will go to a great cause, but money is not really what I'm after. The art must be protected and loved, in safe hands, to be enjoyed by generations. I have a job to do now, a duty to the people," he concluded.

"My respect to you, sir. I wish you well in your project. I think my bag's inside," I said.

We walked inside together, without saying another word, till I retrieved the envelope of money from my bag.

"Contribute this to your cause," I said to Ivan.

"Thank you, Sebastian. I will see you tomorrow, at noon. You will take the best lot of miniatures, and you can enjoy the auction knowing it won't be there to be sold to anyone else," he said, wearing a smile and reaching out to shake my hand.

"Thank you so much," I replied, "and for the Hugo letter as well."

"Idris will drop you off at your hotel," Ivan said, and he laughed again when he noticed my expression fall. "Oh, don't let that one frighten you, my boy. He has a heart of the purest gold. He is like a brother to me, my best friend. In this life, he is the only man I can trust."

I was just about to walk out with Idris when I saw a painting on its back on the reception table, right next to the door.

Ivan caught me looking at it and said, "If Pollock had an heir in the East, it would be the artist behind this painting."

When he turned it over, my mouth fell agape at its unique beauty. The painting in a golden frame resembled an eye, with lashes coming from within, swirling in a vast ocean, all in spectacular yellow and blue contrast. *Is it the sun combined with the sea, giving birth to an eye?* I wondered but didn't know. "This is a real piece of art, art at its best. Is it for sale too?" I asked.

"No. I received it as a gift two days ago. Too bad he doesn't know I am selling everything." He hesitated for a moment, then said, "Sebastian, do you have any engagements to attend tonight?"

"No. I was thinking of taking a tour of the town, maybe having a drink or two enjoying the sea from one of the cafés," I answered.

"Better yet, you will enjoy and experience the sea itself. Rest at your hotel for three hours. At six, we will set sail on my yacht! You will take in the gorgeous horizon view and meet the man behind this painting. He's an Iraqi by the name of Akram Shukri, and he is my guest tonight. The yacht is at the harbor in Trogir, in the third slip after the guard post. Look for *Layali*. It means 'nights' in Arabic, before you ask. I am not sure why I named it that, except that I love the sound of the word."

"I am honored, Ivan," I said.

"Where are you staying?" he asked.

I fiddled with things in my pocket for a moment, then showed him the scrap paper containing the name I'd written down while I was back in Paris. "I've booked a room here," I said.

"Ah, a nice, small place, with a wonderful view. Tell the owner you are a friend of mine," he said as he walked me out.

During the ride, Idris and I talked a bit. I learned that he had been with Ivan for over twenty-eight years. It became obvious during our conversation that he really was a nice guy, Ivan's most loyal companion. Idris apologized for being so tough on me at first. "Ivan has been through a lot," he said, "and I mustn't risk his safety with any strangers. Of course, you are not a stranger anymore, my friend!"

"Be sure to tell your dog that," I jested.

"Max knows a friend when he sees one...or sniffs one," he replied with a smile.

After a short ride, the big man dropped me off at the hotel. I was eager for a little sleep, so I made good use of the large bed in that wonderful room that overlooked the sea, the best room in the whole hotel. "It is all courtesy of Ivan Olic," the hotel manager said when I gave him Ivan's regards.

After I had a two-hour nap, the lady at the front desk gave me a wakeup call, just as I asked. I took a cold bath and dressed in jeans and my floral shirt; I was glad I brought such a breezy garment, even though I did not expect to be on a yacht during my trip. The concierge told me how to get to the right dock, and ten minutes later, I was at the harbor. I figured out which vessel was Ivan's even before I read the name, because Idris was standing on deck. On land, he was huge, and he looked even more monumental aboard that ship.

There was another man near him, staring out at the sea, and I assumed it was the artist, Akram.

"Welcome to *Layali*," *Ivan said as I climbed aboard.* "She has been with me for ten years now, but I must give her up as well. Not tonight though. Tonight, we shall enjoy a sail!"

"Twelve," Idris corrected.

"Twelve? Yes, twelve years is right. She's my eighty-foot pearl beauty. She's got a nice living room, a decent kitchen, and a dining area for ten on this level. On the lower level are two master rooms and a queen room. Her beam's about four and a half meters. That's my dear friend, enjoying a drink at the end over there. Come. I'll introduce you to Akram," Ivan said, pulling me by the hand.

Akram was a bit shorter than me but elegantly dressed in white trousers and a loose-fitting, off-white shirt. His salt-and-pepper hair was carefully combed to the side, lifted now and then by the breeze rolling in off the water. He had a soft grip when we shook hands, but there was nothing soft about the way he looked at me; it was as if he was looking inside me, delving into my head.

"I love your painting, Mr. Shukri," I complimented. "It's very powerful, very...alive."

"Thank you, Mr. Sebastian. Ivan said you have an eye for art. I imagine you would, after being surrounded by all those wonders at The Louvre for years and years. I am flattered," Akram said in a low voice, wearing a shy smile.

"Tonight mustn't be so formal," Ivan said. "Let's do away with the mister. We will have a taste of a local white wine, very rich and fruity. Would you like a glass, Sebastian?"

"Yes. Thanks."

Seconds later, we were clinking our glasses together, toasting the night and the good company. The yacht took off across the water, with Captain Idris at the help.

"Ivan said you're Iraqi," I said.

"Yes, from Baghdad," Akram replied.

"I've never been there, but I was in Mosul, with an expedition during my last year in college. We stayed for ten days, checked many Assyrian sites. Amazing history, I must say, and all the people were very kind to us."

"Surely you haven't forgotten the culinary delights," Ivan said while offering us some olives. "I have been to Iraq many, many times on business, mainly Basra, in the south. My company was involved in several projects for the ports there. That was where I met Akram for the first time. When was that, Akram, 1971?"

"Yes. I was in Basra that week, giving lectures at the university. I was in the lobby of the hotel having tea when you came complaining about the window not closing properly in your room. The desk clerk was a young guy, maybe a trainee, and he did not speak English any better than you spoke Arabic. I watched the two of you, looking like deaf people trying to speak with hand gestures. Eventually, I felt sorry for both of you and had to intervene," Akram replied with a big smile on his face.

"Akram was one of the pioneers of the expression movement in Iraq, the first Iraqi to be sent abroad to study art. He went to London back in 1931. He was inspired by Pollock when they met during one of his visits to America, and he went into art dipping after that. As you know, I've always been an art connoisseur, so that chance meeting was too good to be true. We've rendezvoused many times over the years, in Baghdad, Basra, London, Zagreb, Belgrade, Paris, and here. Friendships, old and new. Let's drink to that!" Ivan said, lifting his glass for us all to join him in another toast.

We all sat down on the white leather cushions scattered about. We enjoyed the natural spectacle of the sea, the sunset, and the islands we passed.

"You know, there are around 1,000 islands on the Adriatic, but only about 50 are really habitable. We'll have dinner later at Hvar, one of the biggest and most beautiful of all the islands."

As we talked and got to know each other, I noticed that Akram often drifted away from our conversations, as if he was somewhere else. Since he was an artist, I was compelled to ask him about how he got his start, about his vision as a creator of art. So, after my third glass of excellent white wine, I sat beside him and found the courage. "Why do you paint, Akram?" I asked. "What—"

"Close your eyes, Sebastian," he said, stopping me. "Just for a minute, close them and tell me what you see."

I did as he asked and answered, "Nothing, just black."

He tilted my head a bit to the west. "Open them now and find the blessing of vision. This abundance, the explosion, the mixture of colors, the movement, life passing by... See the sun setting? What colors can you find in the sea? Surely there are blue and gray, but don't you also see that darker gray, light green, even black? Look at the hues of the sun drowning in the sea, melting in oranges, reds, purples. Look at those trees over there. Look at the waves, at me, at your hands, the eyes of your friends. Now, must you still ask me why I paint?" Akram replied. He then left me and walked to the tip of the yacht to enjoy the sunset and the breeze.

"Artists," I mumbled to myself.

We had dinner at a lovely hilltop restaurant on the beautiful Island of Hvar, so high up that we could see the lights of the town and the church steeples below. I found my appetite when I was served a big plate of grilled lobster, shrimp, sea bass, and cuttlefish, with fresh-cut lemon wedges.

"The food is amazing, and you are always such a great host, Ivan," Akram said, looking admiringly at his friend.

"Delicious indeed," I parroted, thanking the man for a great meal.

"I miss the Mazqouf, though, Akram. No one grills fish better," Ivan said.

"Baghdad is your second home. Visit anytime. That goes for you as well, Sebastian," Akram offered.

"I appreciate that, but I doubt I'll be doing much traveling with my project underway. Plus, I can't leave my mother for long," I said. I then turned to Ivan. "Speaking of my mother, is there any way I can call her? I haven't spoken to her all day."

"Yes, of course. Aren't you going back tomorrow though?"

"Yes, but I always call her daily while I'm abroad. She worries, and I worry about her too," I replied.

"Good on you. My children haven't called me in over six months. Anyway, just go inside and tell Luka you want to use the phone."

My mother picked up on the second ring and was quick to tell me she was doing well. " Mrs. André is going to spend the night with me," she said. She was also very happy to hear my news about my wonderful visit. She sounded ten years younger, and she said she couldn't wait to open our new gallery. "Oh, Ana called," she mentioned. "She asked about you, and I hope you don't mind that I shared our good news with her."

As soon as I hung up with her, I called Ana at her apartment. I knew it was close to evening there, so I feared she might not answer, but she finally picked up.

"Ana, it's Sebastian. Can you hear me?" I said as the line filled with static.

"Sebastian! Your mother said you are somewhere in the Adriatic. I am so happy to hear your plans. It is your time to shine."

"Thanks. I've been on a yacht all evening, out on the sea. I've been thinking about you, and when my mother said you called, I had to speak to you."

"A yacht on the sea? Oh, how I wish I was there with you. I love the ocean. I can imagine it, the two of us floating out there, you serenading me under the moonlight with that guitar. I can't think of anything better. When your mother told me about the gallery, I picked up a canvas. I'm going to paint something for you, and I'll make sure it ships in time for your grand opening. You always inspire me, Sebastian, always."

"Thanks, Ana, my Red Queen. I… Hmm…" I said, then trailed off, unable to finish because I was so overcome with emotion.

"Me, too, Sebastian. Me too," she said sweetly, then hung up.

We sailed back slowly, and Idris even let me take the wheel for a brief time. When he felt I was a bit tipsy, he gave me a look, and I respectfully stepped down. It would not be wise to argue with the captain, and when the captain was a man of such size, that would have been suicidal.

At noon the next day, I donned my other white shirt and the same suit I'd worn the day before. I hurried to the auction, which was being held less than a ten-minute walk from my hotel.

Ivan had booked a room in the city hall. The place was nearly packed when I arrived, people pouring in from the early reception I'd missed. I took my place in one of the few remaining empty seats in the back. There were four rows of four chairs on the right and four rows on the right, all facing a small stage with a red curtain at the back, a small wooden podium with a black microphone on top, and a table where I guessed the items would be placed. It looked like a small theater, and everyone was anxious for the show to start.

Ivan sat in the first row, right next to Akram. I recognized a few of the other faces among the attendees. I knew Ruud, who worked for the Rijksmuseum in Amsterdam. There was another man

I'd seen in Florence some years back, though I couldn't remember his name. Matthew Pearce was there, of course, in the front row on the right. I could tell he was surprised by my presence when our eyes met. We exchanged nods.

Apart from those seated, there was a cameraman standing, and Idris also stood, darting his eyes left and right to keep a close eye on everyone present.

At exactly noon, a man dressed in a dark blue pinstriped suit and thick, red tie entered the room and took the stand. *"Buon giorno, tutti!"* he said in a rather roaring voice. "Welcome to the private auction of Signor Olic, in beautiful Trogir, on this sunny day. I am Roberto Chiesa from Lecce. I will be your host today. This is my first auction and, if I perform to your satisfaction, hopefully the start of many."

I could hear some chatter around the room, and I knew what it was all about. *If Salvador Dali saw this man,* I thought, *he'd surely claim him as his son.* The resemblance was striking, absolutely unbelievable. The auctioneer's voice was fitting, and the Italian never lost his contagious smile. I was sure that if he played his cards right, he would become a legend in his field.

"I would like to thank everyone for sending their finance reports in advance," he continued. "All have been checked and verified. You are all free to enjoy your love for art today. Please review the updated list of items for sale. There were a few minor changes from the original list that was sent to you."

As soon as Roberto said that, I quickly perused the list, and I smiled when the lot I was promised was not among the wares up for bid.

"Any lot that falls below the mentioned estimate will be left out, and the bid will be annulled for that lot," Roberto said, explaining the basic rules and guidelines.

After he answered some of the attendees' questions, the Italian instructed that the first lot should be brought out, and the Chinese vases were carefully placed in front of everyone. Roberto banged his gavel on the stand, officially opening the auction, and the cameraman snapped a few shots from the back.

I had never been to an auction before. I focused on every detail, taking it all in and scribbling in my notebook. Small bidding wars broke out, and the bidders tried to keep their expressions to themselves, so as not to give their intentions away. It was like watching a heated game of poker, and there was a certain etiquette about it that I took note of.

One precious lot after another was sold. The clock went to a private collector from Moscow, an old Russian in a black fur hat. The religious books were snatched up by The National Museum of Shanghai; their representative was the only lady in the house. A museum in Ghent took some scrolls. The swords went to a representative from an anonymous collector in Tel Aviv. Nearly everyone took part in the bidding except Matthew, who remained quiet and just stared at Roberto, as expressionless and cold as an iceberg. Then, when the statues came up for bid, that iceberg exploded.

Someone from the Art Institute of Chicago started the bidding at nearly twice the listed price. Then, out of nowhere, Matthew tripled that bid. The whole room went quiet, and all eyes were on him. No one could match that bid, and when more statues were put on the auction block, everyone waited for him to start things off and take charge. As a result, Pearce Gallery scored the next three out of four lots. The Art Institute of Chicago only gained one of Alberto Giacometti's works because Matthew seemed content with the victories he'd already won.

"Well, that was an intense thirty minutes we had," Roberto said, smiling as the last statue was carried away. He then stepped away from the podium.

All eyes followed the auctioneer, confused by his brash departure.

A minute later, the Italian returned with a large easel. "*Scusi mi, tutti*! I wanted to do this one myself, our final set of paintings. Per favore, Signor Dejan, let's begin," he said to the man who'd been handling all the items from the start.

There was some noise in the room, lots of murmuring and whispering as the cameraman took snapshots of the crowd. A war quickly broke out over the first painting of Metzinger, a kerfuffle between Matthew, the older man from Moscow, and The Art institute of Chicago. In the end, the Russian took it, but Matthew got the Renoir, along with Gauguin's painting of a Haitian woman. Henri Matisse's painting went to the guys from Chicago, as Matthew did not even bid for that. It was obvious to all that he was waiting for Titian's work.

Roberto was about to speak when Ivan stood and approached the podium. My friend looked very sharp in his dark gray suit and a black and white checkered tie.

Roberto placed his hand on the microphone. Then, after Ivan whispered a few words in his ear, the auction master nodded and continued, "I must apologize, but Signor Olic has decided not to auction the last piece. I would like to thank everyone for coming. *Ciao tutti e buonasera*," Roberto concluded.

Matthew stared fiercely at Ivan as Idris moved to me and handed me a white envelope.

"What's this?" I whispered.

"Just open it," the friendly giant said.

Inside the envelope was some money, along with a folded note. I quickly unfolded the note and read, under my breath:

Sebastian,

How ironic that I am undertaking a project for the elderly! I aim to open a nicer facility for them than anyone has ever opened before. This is my goal in life from now on. I was touched by your story and the kindness and responsibility you show toward your dear mother. Some things are so precious, worth more to me than all the money in the world. Tiziano's painting is also yours. Take care of it. It's a favorite of mine.

Do pay Mrs. Stanley in Dorchester a visit. You can use part of this money there, for a small Gauguin painting. I will send her word, and she will give it to you. Schmidt knows her.

Good Luck.

Ivan

I folded the note, put it back in the envelope, then stuffed the whole thing in my jacket pocket. I looked over at Ivan, and he smiled at me, as did Akram beside him.

"We should go," Idris whispered, placing his big arm on my shoulder. "Ivan booked a flight for you from Split to Zagreb. Leaves in three hours. From there, you go back to Paris."

I got up and walked slowly out of the room, only to hear someone calling my name as soon as I made it down the stairs.

"Hey, Sebastian!"

I turned and saw no other than Matthew Pearce.

"One question, and please be frank in your answer. Did you guys get the painting in the end?" he asked.

"Us?"

"Yeah, you, The Louvre?" he said in a furious tone, his hands trembling with anger.

"No, not The Louvre. *I* got it," I proudly replied.

"Say again. You?" he asked sarcastically.

"Yes. I have a project of my own," I said.

"A project?" He laughed. "Look, kid, you are just a toad. This art game is an ocean, not a pond near your grandmother's place. You are making a mistake. You are...nothing," he arrogantly scolded before he walked away.

I was about to respond, but Idris motioned for me to move along. Then, as soon as we were in the car, the man bellowed a laugh as big as he was.

"What?" I said.

"A toad. Not so much. You will be so big one day. This man will have nightmares of you every night," he said as he continued chuckling.

"What makes you say that?" I asked, confused.

"Twenty-three years ago, I saw the same thing happen to Ivan when we were in Belgrade for a meeting. A millionaire named Boris belittled him. Ten years later, Ivan took over all that man's business, all over the world. It is the circle of life," he said and laughed again.

"The circle of life," I repeated, then chuckled with him. "I hope lightning will strike twice!"

The first thing I did when I arrived home, was to hang Victor Hugo's framed letter over my late grandfather's bed. "You will have good company from now on," I said to both the letter and my grandfather's memory, then walked out and closed the door behind me.

Chapter Five

I was very happy with all the progress made in just four weeks. I had secured a manageable rent agreement with Madam Isabelle, Monsieur Daniel's eldest daughter, a two-year contract with payments made on a quarterly basis. I explained to them what changes I planned to make in the place, and they seemed happy with it. Isabelle and her brother lived in Montreal, and it was a relief to them to find a renter so quickly, especially one they'd known for years. Thus, the deal was inked, and everyone was pleased.

I also got the necessary approval and permits from the municipality and committees. Most importantly, I attained my gallery license, in the name of Allure Gallerie.

By the end of the first two-hour meeting with the contractor, he knew exactly what was needed. We had taken the time to design the layout with an engineer who was a close friend of Professor Schmidt's. Monsieur Daniel's old library was an L-shaped open space that occupied the corner at the intersection of two streets. We decided that the entrance door would be on the bigger side, facing the main street, a stained glass door in every color available. That door would lead to a small, open seating area, where I would house a small library of books and catalogs related to art and my collections. Of course there would be two bathrooms, one for women and the other for men, both wheelchair accessible, on the left side of the entrance. I even thought about putting a gift shop in that area in the future.

The front would then split into two rooms of equal size, instead of just one, as it did in the past. A small wall would have to be constructed in the middle to separate the two galleries where I would temporarily display works from different artists each week. Those two galleries would open to a smaller room that would be home to my permanent pieces, my treasury. A small office with a conference table large enough to seat four would be built next to the main gallery on the left. The office area would lead to a stainless steel safe room where valuable artwork could be stored; I would invest the most in that room, to make sure it was very secure.

When the contractor began his work, he promised to deliver within two months, exactly three weeks before my grand opening. Thanks to Professor Schmidt's keen negotiation skills, the expenses were kept under control.

Once the plans for the premises were understood and underway, the really hard work began. I had to embark on the search for unique, undiscovered art, for those hidden gems that deserved a chance to shine. We distributed brochures to every art university campus, art club, café, and other places where inspired artists like to spend their time. We also took out several advertisements in newspapers all over France, making sure to mention that there was a fresh opportunity to display work at Allure Gallerie, a new gallery in Le Marais in Paris. We made sure to mention that there was space for artists who'd never held an exhibition in the past.

In the first three days, we had sixty-four calls. Within 10 days, the incoming rings numbered over 180, as word about the opportunity started circulating. When we hit 200 calls, we began our process of selection. At the start, we hoped to find twenty suitable artists, so we could showcase two a week. The exception would be a solo exhibition the first week, the icing on the cake, so that artist had to be good. Creative individuals came to us from as far as Marseille, some carrying only one painting and others loaded down with over ten.

Professor Schmidt and I met the artists at his place during the weekdays, and we spoke to twenty of them a day. Because we had so many artists to meet, we started at ten in the mornings. Before that, I spent a few hours with the carpenters and laborers at the gallery, checking on the progress and giving the contractor my notes when necessary. Then, I'd spend the rest of the day at the professor's place, till about four in the afternoon.

The professor made sure to set his living room up nicely, with all the shades open for extra light. I sat on his brown leather sofa, and the professor always chose his favorite rocking chair. We set up an easel in the middle of the room, with a chair next to it for the artists to sit on. We began the interviews by speaking with each artist for a few minutes, in an attempt to understand their personality. We always offered a glass of wine or some coffee to put them at ease. Then, we asked the artists to display their work and tell us a little about it.

We did our best to make it easy for them, to give it a casual, relaxed feel, but with Professor Schmidt's cane always at his side, I doubted it was too comfortable for anyone. Many knew who the man was, and his reputation spoke for itself. In all, each interview lasted about half an hour, but some artists were with us for only a few minutes.

After an exhausting day of meetings, we enjoyed taking long walks in the Jardin des Tuileries, then settled down on one of the benches, facing our inspiration The Louvre. A short while later, I had to go home to relieve Mrs. André, who had agreed to continue caring for my mother till the gallery opened. Sometimes Antoine and Émilie joined us for drinks, and my mother was always thrilled to see their newborn daughter.

I signed some papers, and the kind lady behind the post office desk went into the back room and gathered a large package and a cardboard tube. I was so thrilled that my paintings had made a safe journey from Dorchester. I was beginning to worry that I wouldn't receive them on time for Professor Schmidt and I to prepare them for the opening, but now they were finally in my hands, finally mine, after being with Mrs. Stanley for more than forty years.

My trip to Dorchester a month earlier was a bit tiring but fruitful. After I told Professor Schmidt about the note Ivan gave me, he made sure to tell me all he knew about Mrs. Stanley. I learned that she was married at the age of 19 to a major in the British Royal Airforce, a son of a lord in Dorchester. Major Stanley was the only heir of an extremely wealthy family who owned land as far as the eye could see. When her poor husband met his doom when his plane was shot down over France, Mrs. Stanley inherited it all, as they had no children. She became a widow at the age of 41, and she never remarried and remained in the family estate. The Stanleys loved art, and everything they owned was passed on to her, a collection of over 100 treasures.

Through the years, Mrs. Stanley donated most of those valuable paintings to museums all over Europe, precious pieces by Van Gogh, Whistler, Manet, Francisco Goya. The Louvre was only one of the beneficiaries of her generosity. Professor Schmidt met her once at a special dinner arranged in her honor back in 1957.

As soon as I called, Mrs. Stanley kindly invited me to her place. I booked the flight the next day. The trip to London was an easy one, but once I arrived there, I encountered one disaster after another for me. That rainy day, the train stopped at Southampton because some workers were on strike, so there were no more trains to Dorchester for the day. I asked around and was advised to take a bus. From the bus station, I hopped in a cab that broke down five miles away from Mrs. Stanley's residence. I waited for a quarter-hour, but when I saw no sign of anyone who could help, I decided to walk. Minutes later, the clouds darkened, and rain started splashing down on me from every direction. It was the worst rain I'd ever seen, and by the time I reached her place, I was soaked to the bone and covered in mud from head to toe.

I was embarrassed by my appearance, about looking so dilapidated on the doorstep of such an extravagant place, but the old lady just laughed when she saw me.

"That's the weather in Dorset for you. You'd better come inside, before you catch pneumonia," she said.

"I did bring some spare clothes. I can change," I said after I explained all the misfortunes of my journey.

"Nonsense!" Mrs. Stanley said. "Keep your clothes for your trip back. You never know how much it's going to rain in Dorset." She then asked her butler to get me some dry clothes.

I took a warm bath and dressed in what was given to me. To my surprise, the brown trousers were just about a perfect fit, as was the long-sleeved, off-white shirt. I slid my feet into the slippers she provided, then joined my hostess again.

Mrs. Stanley was a small, thin woman, and her white hair was cut very short, like a man's. She was wearing a red dress and a beautiful ruby and diamond necklace that covered most of her wrinkled neck. Her nails were painted red as well. She was extremely elegant and never seemed to lose the nice smile on her face.

"Ivan said you are an ambitious art lover, not at all shy about it," she began. "I see now that he must not have exaggerated, if you traveled all the way out here in this horrible weather," the wrinkled woman said.

"Thank you for receiving me," I said. "I'm sorry about the short notice, but I am running out of time to nail down a collection before my gallery opens."

"Well, I won't keep you waiting. Have your tea, and then we will go to the attic."

Mrs. Stanley told me that she had only had a few things left, including some portraits of her husband, herself, and her parents. She said she'd already donated nearly everything else and sold a few at auctions. The Matisse painting Ivan sold was one of those. "I only have a few things remaining. I wanted to give them to Ivan to auction, as my contribution to his project for the elderly, but the pieces need some work. See, one day, we endured heavy rain like this storm today, and the roof in the dining area where they were kept sprang a leak. Sadly, some of the paintings suffered slight water damage." She paused and winced, as if it pained her to tell me about it. Then she continued, "I promised this Cezanne to my butler. He's always adored it. You can have a look at those two small ones by Gauguin though. Unfortunately, the paint on the one on the right is starting to crack. I don't know if you'd be interested in that one."

I looked carefully at both paintings. They'd seen better times, and as well as the damage to the paintings themselves, one of the frames was broken beyond repair. Still, I was sure I could put them to good use. "I will take them both," I told Mrs. Stanley. "I can pay six or seven—"

"Did Ivan take your money?" she cut in.

"No, but—"

"But nothing! If Ivan would not take money from you, why should I?" She paused and smirked a bit. "Now think carefully before you say another word, lad. I might take a refusal of my generosity as an insult, and my wrath on you would make the rainy day in Dorset seem like a sunny one!" She continued smiling, but there was a seriousness in her tone that made me sure she meant every word. After all, she'd lived over thirty years on her own, and she had the same subtle strength about her that I saw in my own mother.

"The official grand opening is December 4, and I'd be honored by your presence," I said.

She was clearly pleased with my carefully chosen words. "Count me in," the old lady said.

Unlike my trip from Paris, the return trek was pleasant, and I felt a deep satisfaction that things were starting to come together to fulfill my dream of having my own gallery.

Now, a month later, I was carrying those two Gauguins in my own hands, and I hurried from the post office to Professor Schmidt's place so I could work on them immediately. They needed a lot of loving care, and I was eager to give it to them.

I knew it would be difficult to restore the paintings, but it would not be an impossible feat, especially for the two of us. We'd been working on art restoration for many years, hundreds of them between us.

"Tell your mother to whip up some of that chicken and mushroom soup tonight," the professor said as soon as he had his first look at the paintings. "We have a lot of work ahead of us, and we'll do it at your place in the evenings. Why, by the time we are finished, these will be like new. Gauguin himself would give us a standing ovation."

"If you say so," I said.

"I do! Now, let's meet some more artists, shall we? The first has already arrived," he said, looking out his window.

One after another, the artists came, and we enjoyed meeting them all.

The contractor proved true to his word and finished everything early, with three weeks to go. He handed the keys over and said, "We've done what we can. The rest is up to you."

I decided that the main gallery would look best with red carpet and walls painted in dark gray. The rest of the floors would be white marble.

There would be ten paintings in the main room: the two Gauguins brought back to life; the five miniatures of Ruben and Eyck; Ana's painting, which I would receive soon; Titian's mythological wonder; and the surprise gift I got from Akram Shukri, *The Eye*. Of course I was hysterical when I received that painting with Ivan's shipment.

Schmidt was very happy with all that had been done, but he was excited when it was his turn to intervene.

"Proper lighting is the path to a great painting," he had always said, and he was going to make sure every painting we displayed was properly illuminated. He suggested that two crystal chandeliers should be placed in the main room. "The contrast of the gray walls, red carpet, and twenty-four candle lights of the chandeliers will be sufficient," he explained. The other two galleries were fitted with six suspending lamps and twenty spotlights between them.

"Perhaps we should use different lamps, vary them from one show to the other," I suggested.

"As long as the power and direction of the lights stays the same, I think that's a great idea," Schmidt said.

There was a big shop that sold lamps of various types near Place des Vosges, a store Émilie had recommended. I paid them a visit just before noon and spent over an hour there. With the spare money I had on hand, I bought six sets of three suspending lamps. The owner promised to send them to the gallery the next day. I wanted to celebrate my purchase with Émilie, with the best bottle of red wine I could find. My friend deserved it, because she'd done so much for me. She'd even managed to land me a twenty-minute radio interview on a program related to art, about a week before the opening. She'd also arranged for Professor Schmidt to be interviewed for *Le Monde* newspaper. Her years of work in the PR Department at her company put her in contact with a huge network of people, and that was a great asset to me.

I checked my watch. The café where we were supposed to meet was a ten-minute walk away, and I was already five minutes late. With that in mind, I ran from one end of Place des Vosges to the other. Luckily, there were not many people around, since the day was surprisingly cold, far chillier than usual for mid-November. There were a few out walking their dogs, but I just carefully hurried around them, because I knew Émilie was a very prompt person who hated to wait. I nearly fell at one point, due to a loose shoelace that I had to sit down on a bench to tie.

Crack!

The noise startled me, and I turned around to see a tall man in a fully buttoned, dark gray raincoat and sports shoes, breaking a small branch from a tree about ten feet away. He had long hair and an untidy, unshaven beard. He carried the twig over to a place where there were several cans scattered on the ground, near an easel with a canvas on it. He then picked up a brush with his left hand, stuck it in one of the cans, and stroked it across the canvas a few times.

"Hmm. Just another wannabe painter," I said to myself as I stood and started to walk away, eager to meet Émilie. My curiosity got the best of me, though, so I turned to look at him again.

This time, he was holding the brush with his right hand, and he seemed just as comfortable painting the canvas that way.

Was it left at first or right? I thought, confused. I sat down on a bench a little closer to him. I was sure Émilie would understand if she had to wait just a little bit longer.

As I sat and quietly watched, he continued shifting the brush from one hand to the other. He painted the left side of the painting with his right hand and the right side of the painting with his left. Then, after turning the painting upside down a few times, the weird man pulled a pocket knife out of his jacket. That was a bit shocking, but he only used it to cut small pieces of wood from the twig he'd broken off the tree. He made a chunk of small pieces, dipped them in another can full of a brownish color, then picked a thinner brush, stuck it in, and started making straight strokes.

"What is he doing?" I asked, a little too loudly, though he didn't bother to answer me.

Next, he tore some grass out of the ground and started to stick the blades to the wet paint on the canvas.

That was enough craziness for me, so I stood and walked nearer, to see what he was up to. When I was within a few feet, there was only one thing I could say: "Damn."

Never in my life had I seen artwork like that. The colors on the left side of the painting seemed to swirl in my eyes. A river ran through the middle, and the right side of the painting was a mirror of the left, only in dull colors. It was the same part of a city, on both banks of a river, identical but different, drawn by two different hands. I moved closer to look at it and saw that the trunks of the trees were brown and full of the wood chips. The grass was a shade of green I'd never seen before; it was a mix of what was inside the can and the actual grass he had cut. The buildings on the banks were a mix of grays, whites, and some small pieces of rocks he'd crushed. The painting was full of layers, not only of paint but of nature as well. It was even more fascinating than the work by the Mexican artist I'd met in Miami.

Out of the 200 artists who visited us, Professor Schmidt, and I had chosen our twenty artists. All of our selections were great, but I still did not see any particular one of them as worthy of being the opening act for my gallery. I needed something beyond great; I needed sensational, a revolution. When I saw that man painting with chunks of nature, I knew I was looking at just that.

"Bonjour, monsieur," I said.

For a response, the painter turned around and simply nodded.

"Great work," I said.

Again, he offered me no verbal answer.

"I am Sebastian," I introduced, hoping to start a conversation.

"No Frank," he finally replied, in a heavy accent.

"No, Frank? Ah, you don't speak Francais. English? Italiano, Español? "

"No, no," he said, shaking his head. "Türkçe, Deutsch."

"Deutsch? Thank God," I said, and I suddenly could not wait for Professor Schmidt to meet the guy. "Sebastian," I repeated and offered my hand.

"Hakan," he replied, shaking it.

I pointed at the painting and gave him a thumbs-up. "Bravo!" I said.

"Marci," he replied, albeit somewhat poorly. He clearly knew no French, but I didn't care, as his work spoke for him, in a language anyone could understand.

I explained as much as I could with words and hand gestures, trying to make him understand just how much I loved his work, that it was worth good money, and that my German friend would equally adore it. I also did my best to invite him out for a meal.

Finally, Hakan took the canvas off the easel and started packing up his supplies.

I jumped in to help, picking up the brushes, cans, and everything else as fast as I could. Once both of our hands were full, I led the way to the café. I was half an hour late, and I knew I was in trouble, but the excuse was walking with me.

Émilie was staring at the small TV when I arrived. She had a cigarette in one hand and a cup of coffee in the other. She looked surprised when she saw me, especially since I was carrying a box, walking next to tall, bearded, rather scruffy-looking man she'd never seen before.

"Sorry, dear, for being late, but... Well, something just happened out of nowhere," I said as I kissed her.

"Sebastian, I have known you since you hit puberty, and you still surprise me every day. It's one thing that you're thirty minutes late. It's another that you bring a stranger. Who is this?" she whispered in my ear.

"Hakan, Émilie," I said, introducing them both to each other.

"Hello, Hakan. How are you?" she politely asked.

Hakan smiled and looked at me, as if he was waiting for me to tell her something.

"Émilie, I found Hakan painting in Place des Vosges. He doesn't speak French, only German. Hey, do you have a car?" I asked.

"A car?" she said, looking kindly at Hakan.

"Yes. I'd like to go to Professor Schmidt's place."

"Now? But you just got here, and—"

Before she could finish, I took the painting from Hakan, and showed it to her. "Yes, now, Émilie," I said.

"Oh! Of course, right away," she said, unable to take her eyes off his work. "My car is parked out there on the left, the blue Peugeot. I sold the red one."

"Great. You take Hakan with you. I'll just grab some sandwiches and croissants for us."

Around three, we arrived at Professor Schmidt's place.

The professor was in his robe when he opened the door. "Is there a party at my home that I am not aware off? Welcome, Émilie," he said, then kissed her while rearranging his robe. "Sebastian, I will have a word with you later about this," he boomed before inviting us in.

"Sorry to wake you, Professor. I know it has been only a few days since you started sleeping like a retiree once again, but I want you to meet Hakan." I then hustled into the living room, opened the easel, and placed Hakan's painting on it. "He's all yours, Professor. He only speaks three or four words of French, but he knows German."

"German, eh?" The professor looked at the painting, then looked at Hakan. He looked at the painting again, then looked at Hakan once more. Then, he pulled Hakan over to the sofa and sat beside him. There, the two of them engaged in a half-hour conversation in German.

Émilie and I just stared, not uttering a word, as the two men talked and laughed. I knew the professor well; once he was on a roll, the last thing he wanted was an interference.

"I must have a bath, and then we will drive to Hakan's place," he finally said. "He has over twenty paintings there. In the meantime, he is hungry. Why are you hoarding all those sandwiches instead of eating them? Do you want our new star to starve to death?"

"You were talking this whole time!" I said. "Besides, it's *your* home, Professor, and you haven't offered your guest anything to drink. Where is that good wine of yours?" I asked as I took the food out and passed the cheese sandwich to Hakan.

"We've got ourselves a rare artist here, a man who doesn't drink, doesn't smoke. Émilie, would you be so kind as to fetch him some fresh orange juice from the refrigerator? Hakan says he is staying near The Basilica of Saint Denis. I will tell you all about him on the way," Professor Schmidt said.

"Twenty paintings? Émilie, did you hear that? You've been all over me for the past two weeks, afraid I wouldn't be ready for the radio program or the gallery, with an opening act. I think that's settled now," I said, looking at Hakan, who had already finished the sandwich I'd passed to him a minute ago.

With the professor acting as our translator, we soon learned that Hakan had been in Paris for three months. He came from Essen, Germany, and he was raised in a broken home. Both of his parents ended up in Germany from Turkey after World War II, and both were jobless, so the family was drowning in poverty. He had a twin sister, and the siblings had been forced to work in the streets since childhood, mainly as beggars. His sister married a French man of Turkish descent who owned a butchery in Paris. Seval sent for her brother after she settled in Paris, hoping Hakan would work at his brother-in-law's shop, but Hakan felt the man was taking advantage of him, and he quit the job after three weeks. Now, he worked six nights a week at a steel factory.

Hakan resided with four other men in a small place on the third floor of an old building, still going through everyday life in harsh conditions. He had no idea how dramatically his life was about to change because of his rare talent.

Hakan and I put his precious paintings in two old boxes. He packed his meager belongings in a small, worn shoulder bag. He then bid farewell to his roommates, who had no idea what was going on. After that, we made our way back to the professor's home, where Hakan would stay for a while.

Émilie dropped us off and left right away, certain that Antoine would be furious with her for being gone so long. "I should have been home an hour ago. As happy as Antoine is with our little princess, he can only handle her for a short time. Oh well. Fathers will be fathers, I suppose," she said before she left.

Professor Schmidt and I placed the twenty-one paintings on the floor and examined each of them.

"Look at those colors. Have you ever seen anything like them?" I asked. "Please ask our friend how he does that."

Again, the men engaged in a long, German conversation. Hakan's voice was heavy, and he was very animated with his hands as he spoke. All the while, the professor just listened carefully, nodding in admiration.

"He said he's been playing with colors as long as he can remember. Whenever his parents fought, he and his sister escaped the shouting by going to a park near their home, their haven. His sister Seval played with her only doll, but Hakan spent that time enjoying his watercolors. Don't ask me where he got them."

"But the colors. They're so...vibrant," I said.

"When he was little, he learned to add some grass to the green, squeeze orange in the red, purple in the orange, and add a bit of mud to the brown. You can guess the rest. As he grew older, he experimented more and more. He boiled grass and squeezed it to extract whatever color he could. He thickened the mud by boiling it. He added honey and glue, and he poured all those mixtures into big cans of different colors, never using a palette. Then he started adding crushed stone, coal... The list goes on. He said he learned a new tactic every day."

"Honey, mud, and coal? Wow! That's almost too much to comprehend, so unique. I say we should leave Hakan's secrets to him. Magicians should never tell their tricks after all! What about the ambidexterity though? Why both hands...and how? Also, why is the right half in darks, grays, blacks, and whites, while the left is such an extravaganza of colors? Why the contradiction? Why a river in the middle of all his paintings? A city, two moons, animals, or faces... It's always a mirror image on both sides of a river," I said, looking at once canvas after another.

"Who are you talking to, Sebastian? Of course I already asked him about that," Professor Schmidt replied, pointing his cane at me. "He says water is always the source of life. Without it, there is no meaning to anything. As for the reason behind his style of right and left, Hakan says that when he paints, his eyes look straight at the canvas ahead, or the world if I was to translate what he used when mentioning the canvas. He says his eyes don't deviate a bit. Each one looks into its own half. His eyesight interprets the world only half in color. This is life for him, happy and sad."

I stood up and kissed the guy on his head, overcome with emotion. "Hakan, oh Hakan. Professor, tell him that the painting he was drawing at the park... Please ask him to finish it, and I will consider it a gift from him. It will be in my permanent display after the show," I said enthusiastically.

Over the next two weeks, we did the best we could to spread the word about Hakan among those we knew. Professor Schmidt took the artist to his tailor, and several suits were custom made to fit his large physique. The funny thing was that Hakan preferred them all to be in black.

As for his own grooming, Hakan just trimmed his black beard and left his hair as it was, in his own scraggly style. We didn't mind, because we didn't want to change him too much. He learned a few more words in French, and he endured many of Professor

Schmidt's lectures about life and art. *Some habits never die,* I thought with a smile when I heard him enlightening Hakan with on one of his many speeches, even though I couldn't understand a word of it in German.

During the radio interview, Professor Schmidt and I talked about the paintings that would be included in our permanent display. We talked about the history behind Tiziano's work, Gauguin's brilliance, and Ruben and Eyck's magical, detailed art. We discussed Akram's *The Eye,* and we made sure to mention Ana's flaming trees. The biggest painting in our collection measured fifty by seventy inches; the last painting I received drew oohs and ahs from Professor Schmidt and me the moment we opened the big crate.

We concluded our interview by talking about the highlight of the opening. "It will be the first solo exhibition of an inspired creator of rare, raw art. His name is Hakan, and while he may have been poor in life, his talent is rich, a must-see."

The interview caught the interest of many Parisians, and the article in *Le Monde* made us the talk of the town, indeed of the whole country. Before we knew it, our grand opening was just a week away, and we were not the only ones who were excited about it.

Chapter Six

My mother dressed in a beautiful, long, silky white dress and accessorized with her three-layered pearl necklace and diamond ring, and I were almost the first to arrive at the gallery at nine a.m. The catering team Émilie recommended arrived only a few minutes before us and were already offloading their supplies just outside the door. The three young waiters, two women, and a man were elegantly dressed in white and black. Their supervisor, Madam Marianne, was a classy woman with short, black hair, likely in her fifties and dressed in a knee-length, dark blue dress with gold buttons.

"Bonjour! Everyone ready for today? I need nonstop energy today, nonstop. I want all our visitors to be happy and well taken care off," I announced as I unlocked the door and helped them carry their boxes inside.

"Bien sur, monsieur," Madam Marianne replied with a big smile on her face, looking proudly at her capable team.

After she spoke with her staff for a few minutes, they moved straight to their work, like busy bees. Within moments, they had the whole place set up. Five tall black tables were placed in the front area, each topped with a crystal ashtray and a silver napkin holder.

Smoking would be allowed in the front area only, as we couldn't risk any damage to the paintings inside.

Beautifully engraved crystal glasses, cutlery, and handmade, rectangular aluminum serving trays were all carefully organized.

The small bar was set up the day prior. The young garcon would be stationed behind it, and the two ladies would be in charge of serving the various snacks like olives, dried tomatoes, cheese, and drinks to all the guests.

The evening before the grand opening, before going out to dinner, Antoine and I filled the bar with drinks. We bought twelve bottles of Veuve Clicquot champagne and twenty bottles each of cabernet sauvignon red wine and chardonnay. We also made sure to pick up dozens of cartons of Perrier and Evian water, as well as orange and apple juice and cola, so we could satisfy all tastes.

My mother joined me in her wheelchair, and we moved swiftly through the place to make sure everything was going as planned. The spiral black and white lamps we'd specifically selected for the opening day worked beautifully, the paintings were in place, and everything was neat, tidy, and spotless.

Ten minutes later, Antoine showed up, dressed in uncharacteristically elegant style. He was followed by Émilie and her cousin, the violinist. Weeks earlier, my friend had bragged and bragged about Jannette's musical talent. "She's the best in her class. She'll surely play at the Opera Garnier someday," she said. "Please let her entertain during your opening, Sebastian."

I thought about it only briefly before I agreed. "It will be a great opportunity for her, as she will be seen by many, and it will be something new and good for the gallery as well," I said.

After they arrived, Ivan, Akram, and Idris showed up. I'd enjoyed dinner with them the night before, and I was extremely happy to see them. Truly, I wouldn't have gotten to where I was without them, especially Ivan. I introduced them to my mother, Antoine, and Émilie. I'd already told my loved ones how huge Idris was, but until the moment he showed up, they never totally believed me.

Professor Schmidt and Hakan arrived at half-past ten a.m. Hakan was in his black suit and the professor in a blue one. Both were wearing white shirts and red ties that matched my own, as we'd agreed on that part of our ensemble the day before.

A few minutes later, a black limousine pulled up to the curb outside, and the chauffer opened the door for Mrs. Stanley to get out. She was gorgeous in her long, turquoise dress and black fur jacket and matching hat.

"Welcome, Mrs. Stanley, to my Allure Gallerie," I said when I rushed over to greet her, pushing my mother in her wheelchair in front of me.

"You know what was happening in Dorset yesterday when I left?" she asked as I lifted her hand to apply a friendly kiss to the top of it. "Raining, of course!"

"Well, it isn't here in sunny Paris!" I replied, grinning. "I'm beyond delighted that you're here, and I'd like to introduce you to my mother."

She peered down at the lady in the wheelchair. "Oh, now I see where you got those good looks, my boy," she said.

I smiled, a bit embarrassed. "Yes, everyone says I inherited my hazel eyes from her, but I think that's about as far as the resemblance goes. I certainly don't have the same pretty smile as you two ladies."

"Nonsense," she said.

"Do come inside," I suggested. "Many of your friends are here, and I'm sure you won't believe what we were able to accomplish with your Gauguin paintings."

"*Your* paintings, Sebastian, *yours,*" she corrected as she stepped inside.

Just an hour before show time, I called everyone close to me. "I want to personally thank you all for being here," I announced. "You have no idea how much it means to me. I hope you all have a great day." I then turned to the catering staff. "Ladies, please bring us some champagne.

Once everyone had their flutes of champagne, we raised them in the air.

"Let the glorious grand opening begin!" I said, smiling at all the lovely faces.

After finishing their first drinks, Ivan, Akram, and Schmidt sat together to have some wine. Idris, meanwhile, engaged in some talk with my mother and Mrs. Stanley. Hakan reviewed and examined his paintings, reciting a few words here and there to practice his French a bit. Antoine, Émilie, Jannette, and I discussed what music should be played, and in the end, we settled on Strauss and Vivaldi.

By eleven thirty, a few people had gathered outside the gallery, waiting for the doors to open. Ten minutes later, the crowd was much bigger and much louder, practically begging to get in.

"There are dozens of them, Sebastian," my mother said, peeking around the curtain.

Idris quickly stood and opened the door. "Dix minutes," the big man said, darting his stern eyes left and right. When the masses silenced, he closed it behind them.

I could not blame them for hushing when they caught sight of the giant. *Good thing he did not bring that dog of his. It may have scared some of them away altogether,* I thought.

"The line stretches 'round the corner," he said to me as he locked the door. "More and more keep coming."

"Already?" I asked in disbelief, looking down at my wristwatch. "How will we manage so many at the same time? It is very important that every guest feels important and can take his or her time with each painting. We need to think this through," I said, worried.

"Sebastian, just relax and enjoy yourself. Look at Idris. You know he can handle anything," Ivan said, clapping his big friend on his humongous shoulder.

"I will make sure there are not too many at once. The weather is great. I will do crowd control from outdoors," Idris offered.

"But how will you know how many—" I began to protest.

The big man gave me a look and held a hand up to stop me, calmly pulled out a notebook and pen, and stepped out the door.

Three minutes later, at noon right on the dot, I nodded to let him know we were ready.

Our guardian rang the big bell twice. "Welcome to Allure Gallerie, ladies and gentlemen," he said in a booming voice, then opened the door for our first round of guests.

As time passed, a steady stream of art admirers filtered through the gallery. I saw thirty, forty, sixty, and more. They thanked us as they left and gave us their best wishes for a bright future. Many promised they would soon return.

For a few minutes, I just stood alone, taking it all in. My gallery was a hit. I struggled to absorb the reality of it as men and women, old and young, took time to speak to Professor Schmidt, with Hakan at his side, about the young man's paintings. A great number of them inquired about the prices. I heard parents explaining Titzano's work to their children. One group spent a long time staring at the Gauguin paintings, and Mrs. Stanley happily indulged their curiosity. A few spoke to Akram about his mesmerizing *The Eye*. My lovely mother, livelier than I'd seen her in a long time, busied herself with registering the names of the attendees and talking and laughing with the guests. A few cameramen snapped photos, and journalists from various papers and magazines interviewed visitors and some of us, with Jannette's amazing violin rendition of Strauss's "Blue Danube" for a backdrop. I had never been happier. In that one moment, I saw all my dreams coming true right in front of me, all but one of them.

That one remaining dream wasn't far behind though. A tall, slim lady sashayed in atop dangerously high black heels. She was dressed in a tight, long, red satin off-the-shoulder gown that revealed her lovely, long neck.

"Ana?" I shouted, shocked to see her.

The minute she saw me, she ran my way, nearly toppling a few guests on her way. "Of course it's me, Sebastian. I wouldn't have missed this for the world. This is your destiny, and the place is just amazing!" she squealed. "There is such a huge crowd outside. By the way, that's Idris out there, isn't it?" she asked before she kissed my lips.

"You are crazy, Ana, my crazy Red Queen. Don't you have a show in Boston in two days?"

"Yes, but two days is lots of time. I must be here to flourish next to my painting. It will help your gallery, my Sebastian. Surely you haven't forgotten how much of a charmer I am," she said, then kissed me again, then again once more.

Despite the fact that I was surrounded by people and beautiful artwork, it was her beauty that most captivated me. I could not take my eyes off her as she floated through the rooms. When she reached Antoine and Émilie, they were equally surprised to see her, and she greeted them with hugs and friendly kisses, albeit not as friendly as the ones she'd given me.

Twenty minutes after five, the last two onlookers left the gallery.

Idris bid the old couple from Toulouse goodbye, then stepped inside. "That's it," he said.

"Well, Mother? How did we do?" I asked.

She took a moment to look at the registrations, then beamed as she answered, "We had 568 visitors today, and 249 of them signed up as members. Hakan, I leave the rest to you." She smiled at the young artist, who surprisingly seemed to understand what she said.

"*Douze, douze,*" he tried in French.

"Yes, twelve of his fifteen paintings were sold," my mother interpreted.

As everyone grew quiet and just stared at me, I walked over to kiss my mother gently on her wrinkled forehead. I then slowly made my way to Professor Schmidt, took him by the hand, grabbed Hakan with the other hand, and raised our arms together.

Instantly, the place erupted in applause.

"Bravo!" shouted Ana.

"Bravooo!" everyone joined in.

"There are a few bottles of wine left, and I see no reason to waste it," I said. "We'll leave here at six thirty and head to the steakhouse in Saint Germain for dinner. You are all invited, with my thanks," I said.

Sensationnel had been feeding me well for years. There were many tiny, wooden tables squeezed closely together on a traditional black and white checkered floor. The walls boasted photographs of the Paris of yesteryear, and the place was romantically lit with candle chandeliers. Jannette was kind enough to serenade us with her violin, and Idris even broke out in song. Despite the broad selection of wines that lined the walls, few of us asked for any, as we'd already had too much at the gallery. The off-key singing was a testament to that.

Everyone ordered steak, medium rare, except for Professor Schmidt, who chose his usual roasted chicken with herbs. For dessert, we all wanted crème brûlée, the chef's signature dish. It was melt-in-our-mouths delicious, a long, sweet note that ended in slight bitterness from the burned sugar. It was as perfect as the rest of our day.

Almost everyone was exhausted and ready to leave after about three hours, but for Ana and me, the night was still young. We dropped my mother off at home, helped her change clothes and get into bed, then hurried out again, this time to our favorite jazz bar.

We danced and kissed, kissed and danced as the music played. Ana was Ana, all natural, sweet, and genuine. The way she talked and the way she thought always came straight from the heart. Something about the way she swirled and twirled her hair took my mind to fantastic places, but I sensed she was very tired. She talked about her trips to San Francisco, Los Angeles, Seattle, and Dallas.

"So many sleepless nights, trying to keep up with all my commitments," she told me. "It is wonderful to exhibit in shows and galleries, but I miss this, Sebastian."

"This?" I questioned.

"Yes. I miss my old life. I miss...you. I miss being myself, painting when I feel like it and not because I'm obliged to. In a few years, after I have made enough money, I will come back here."

"Ana, the minute you say so, I will come get you," I replied, caressing her hair.

A short while later, after she excused herself to the ladies' room, I rushed to prepare a surprise for her. "Ana, this one is for you!" I said with a mic in my hand, sitting on the stage with my guitar. I gave the band a look, then started playing the chords so they could join in on the right beat.

"Unforgettable, that's what you are... Unforgettable, though near or far..." I sang, and when I finished, I saw tears in her eyes.

That night, we made love in the car. Then, I dropped her off at the hotel and bid her farewell.

"Till next time, Ana," I said softly.

"Next time, Sebastian."

My mother woke me at eight a.m. the next day. "I heard you come in around two. Is Ana gone?" she asked.

"She's probably at the airport by now," I replied, hardly able to open my eyes.

"I have never understood this thing between you two. You are like two halves of an apple, yet you are so far from one another. You have such a powerful connection, yet you are separated. Anyway, you must wake up now. It's our second day of work."

The gallery was scheduled to be open six days a week, Tuesdays to Saturdays from nine a.m. to one p.m., then four p.m. to six p.m. On Sundays, we would open from four to six, for two hours only.

I unlocked the steel shutters and pulled them up, then unlocked the door so we could go inside. I turned off the alarm, then made my way to the safe room. I took the ten paintings out to the main room one by one. As always when it came to precious, one-of-a-kind art, Security was a priority.

Really, it was our first day of actual work. My mother was in charge of registrations and the finances, so she would come with me every morning. Professor Schmidt agreed to come in twice a week, on the opening Tuesdays for each new gallery and on Fridays.

It was decided weeks before the opening that there would be an annual membership offered to anyone who wished to attend all the weekly galleries. Those with memberships also had access to the permanent collection, all for a fee of just forty-five francs. My gallery also charged a 40 percent commission on the sales of all artists' works.

I took a gamble the day before, when I priced Hakan's paintings at 5,000 francs each, but it had paid off. What we made on the first day already covered our operating costs for the entire year.

Professor Schmidt and Hakan were dressed more casually this time, still in suits but sans ties. The second day, we saw only thirty visitors, but forty came on the day after that, and all of them signed up for memberships.

By the end of the first week, we had around 500 members. Of course, word-of-mouth and all the publicity from the newspapers and magazines and radio helped a lot. The headlines were amazing: "Elegant, friendly, and worthy," said *Le Monde*. Others were just as complimentary: "Allure Gallerie Is Here!"; "Hakan, the Turkish Sultan"; "Hakan: A New Phase in Art."

Our first exhibition came to an end on Sunday. Later that evening, we wrapped up Hakan's paintings for their new owners. The three that remained after opening day were sold just a few days later, to a scientific attaché at the Turkish Embassy in Paris.

Hakan was happy and could not believe how much money he had made. With it, he even secured a nice place to rent, a great space he could also use as a studio. Better yet, it was only ten minutes away from where the professor lived, and he knew he was always welcomed to visit Schmidt, whenever he wanted. The talented man also had an open invitation to my place.

I knew Hakan was going to make it big, and I was happy we had played a part in helping him find that well-deserved success. I hoped we could do the same for many more skilled artists. I was so impressed with him that I signed a deal with him to display two of his works annually at our gallery, no matter where in the world he was.

"Learn many languages, young friend," Professor Schmidt advised as we shared a toast in the painter's honor. "Life and your art are going to take you to different places from now on. You will always be on top of them!"

Monday, an advertisement appeared in the paper regarding the Tuesday exhibit, which would feature two new artists, a brother and sister from Nice. It would be abstract cubism art at its best, and I couldn't wait to see what the public thought of it.

The siblings had studied art at the University of Barcelona and graduated two years prior. They were inspired by the likes of Picabia, Legar, and Kupka. Most of their paintings depicted complex emotions and sexual acts associated with themes of mechanization and modern life. The duo traveled through many cities in Spain and France, trying their luck, but no one was truly interested. When they saw one of our flyers on a wall while wandering around the University of Provence Aix-Marseille, they called us right away.

It took the professor and I only five minutes to decide that the siblings were a great fit for our gallery. Their use of colors and shapes, coupled with their imagination, won us over instantly. Their three-dimensional output differed a lot from that of one another, but being siblings, they had built-in marketing attraction that we knew the media and adoring public would quickly latch on to and gobble up.

The income from their exhibition did not reach the profit netted by Hakan, as we priced their work at 2,000 francs a piece. Fourteen out of their twenty paintings sold during the week, eight of the sister's and six of the brother's. Nevertheless, it was a mutually beneficial effort, because the siblings brought a new crowd to our gallery, and our memberships increased because of it.

Ten months later, we'd completed thirty exhibitions, sharing sixty new artists with the people in Paris and the many visitors who came from abroad. Cubism, surrealism, landscape art, and arte brut were just some of the styles we displayed. Soon, artists from as far away as Warsaw, Athens, and Casablanca approached us. In time, my gallery became the goal of all inspired artists looking for a break.

Our memberships passed 1,500 within those first few months, and we sold around 400 paintings in that time. The money was great, and we were clearly on a roll, but something was amiss, something I had to discuss with Professor Schmidt.

"Yesterday, I was going through the articles published about the gallery these past few months. More than half of them mention our 'small' permanent collection. I don't like that word, Professor," I said.

"Well, it's a truth you must accept, Sebastian. I share their views but also your concern. You need something more, Sebastian," he wisely acknowledged.

"I know," I said with a sigh. "I've been looking here and there, trying to find a real catch. I've spread the word around too. I spoke to Ana, Antoine, and Émilie. I even called Ivan yesterday, and he is going to ask around for me. I'd like to have something new by the time we celebrate our first anniversary in two months," I replied.

A week later, my dear friend Ivan Olic called me with great news. "Sicily, next Sunday," he said.

"Sicily?"

"Yes. Blandano, on the footsteps of Mount Etna, to be precise. The Ruggeri family has been living there for decades. The father, Paulo, passed away last week, died of a broken heart. See, he was caught in a bitter land dispute with his brother Mario for quite some time. The boys' father left vast vineyards to them both. After his death, they split, and each created their own wines, both of them delicious and successful brands. As their businesses grew, so did the division between them. The were in a legal war over five hectares of land."

"With all due respect and my pity for their loss and heartache," I said, "what does that have to do with art?"

"Well, Sebastian, my contact has informed me that the family legal adviser thinks it is in the best interest of the widow and Paulo's children that all of his precious belongings are sold by Sunday, including some amazing paintings. He fears that Mario might bribe some influential people and try to take the land from Paulo's wife and children. They need to quickly set some cash aside. The auction won't be public, as they want to keep it quiet. Only a few people know about it. How much do you have to spend, Sebastian?"

"Around $70,000. Tell me about the art," I said, now interested.

"There are two. One is a landscape oil painting by Pissarro, and the other is by Modigliani, a painting of a nude gypsy woman smoking. They were purchased in 1933 from Galerie Georges Petit in Paris, when all the gallery assets were auctioned. Sebastian, they are worth at least ten times that much, but I am confident you can get both for that price," Ivan said.

"They sound wonderful, but I'm not sure I really have a chance," I said.

"Don't count on it, my friend. From what I've heard, the few other bidders don't share your taste. They are more interested in...something else."

"Something else?" I asked.

"His stash of weapons," Ivan clarified.

"Damn, Ivan! What are you thinking, sending me to a weapons trafficker in Sicily?" I said furiously and almost hung up on him.

Ivan laughed as he loudly repeated what I'd said, presumably to Idris, who was always beside him. "Calm down now. Paulo had a hobby of collecting weapons of important people. It is said that he owned one of Napoleon's decorative swords, a rifle used by George Washington, and guns that belonged to Hitler, Mussolini, Stalin, and others. Some are even solid gold. Everyone has their eyes on those things, not the paintings," he finished, chuckling even louder.

"Tell Idris not to laugh so hard, or he might burst," I snapped. "What is the exact address of this weapons stash?" I asked, then wrote down all the details very carefully. I reread them to him to make sure I had it all right. "You said it's at three p.m., three days from now, right?"

"Right."

"Okay. I'll be there."

Ever since we opened the gallery, Mrs. André was needed only when I was out of town. When I called her this time, I was glad she was free to take care of my mother on Sunday. I expected I would be back by Monday morning. I then called Paulo's lawyer and shared with him my financial details, and he returned my call a day later and said I was most welcome to attend the auction.

I arrived at Catania airport around one in the afternoon. I was a bit reluctant to take the short transit through Milan, as I'd had bad experiences there in the past. Once, my luggage got lost. Another time, my flight was delayed for more than five hours. However, my only other option was to go to London and catch a direct flight from there to Catania, and that was too risky because I would arrive very close to the auction time, just after two in the afternoon. In the end, I had to opt for Milan. Fortunately, apart from a half-hour delay, everything went fine.

I quickly went to the rental agency and borrowed a two-door blue Fiat 132. I also asked for a map of the island. I got lost once on one of the roads going uphill from the highway of Catania, but after an hour, I was looking at Villa 31, the Ruggeri house.

When a young man asked me something in Italian, I just shouted my name out the car window. A minute later, he opened the red gate and instructed me to park on the left.

There were around four cars parked already, with several men standing next to them, smoking. A short, bald one was the first to greet me when I got out. "I am Dino, the lawyer," he said, shaking my hand repetitively. "You must be Monsieur Sebastian."

"Yes, Signor Dino. I hope I am not too early," I replied while he continued shaking my hand.

"No, no, not at all. We will start in about forty minutes. Let me introduce you to our other guests, and I want you to try the best wine in Sicily, maybe in all Italy," Dino said, finally letting go of my hand.

The other people, all private collectors, didn't speak very much. They all appeared to be Italian, except for one man who had darker skin. His name was Mubarak, and he did not drink the wine that was offered and only asked for water, so I assumed he was an Arab.

Before the auction began, we all sat at a long wooden table that looked out over the vineyards, where a few farmers were harvesting perfectly ripe grapes. I could smell the sweet aroma, and it was a beautiful sight, stretching as far as the eye could see.

At exactly 3 p.m., Dino escorted us inside to a nearly empty room. There were shelves full of plates and cutlery, but there was nothing else in the room except a table with weapons spread out on top of it. I didn't care much to look at those relics, but my heart began to beat rapidly in my chest when I saw the two occupied easels on the right.

"Standing room only in here, gentlemen," Dino said. "I am very sorry for the lackluster setting, but Signor Paulo's death took us all by surprise. We had to set this up rather urgently, for reasons you are aware off.

There is no need to go into private Ruggeri family, so I suggest we start the auction right away. Is everyone okay with that?"

We all nodded.

Dino nodded back at us, then walked back to close the door.

The first item to be put up for auction was a hunting rifle used by George Washington, at a starting price of $10,000. I had no interest in the piece, but I wanted to test the resolve and the poker faces of those around me. Before the Arab could bid, I shouted, "Twelve thousand!" I then studied the competition carefully, examining their eyes and expressions.

"I'll give $14,000," Mubarak said."

I felt that the man to the left of me was about to bid, so I beat him to it with an offer of $18,000. Four bids later, the rather rotund Italian on the far right, Lorenzo, made the purchase for $24,000.

The next item on the block was a 9mm Astra Model 400 pistol previously owned by Franco. Again, I involved myself in the bidding game, just to gain a better understanding of the people I was up against. In the end, the pistol with the solid gold grip went for $48,000, another prize for Lorenzo.

Next, another gun was sold, previously owned by former Egyptian President Gamal Abdel Nasser, and Mubarak was its lucky new owner.

After a half-hour of bidding, I felt I had a good grasp on the men in the room. I shook my head, though, when I saw seven weapons remaining on the table; I was just eager to get to the art.

Dino saw me and smiled. "Let's calm things down a bit, shall we?" he said, still looking at me. "Let's move to the two paintings we have."

I nodded my thanks but didn't make a sound.

Dino shared some details about the first work, by Pissarro. "He was, in his own words, the dean of all impressionists. This is an oil painting of a cold autumn day, created in 1871, a twenty-one-by-twenty-five-inch beauty. For this truly lovely piece of art, we will start the bidding at $7,500."

I waited a bit to see who would attack first. Ten seconds went by, then twenty, before the Italian guy on my left used his annoying, squeaky voice to raise the bid by $1,000. I then offered, "I'll give $9,500." The battle raged on between the two of us for a few minutes, until I was the proud possessor of a Pissarro for only $13,500.

"Next is a stunning piece, Modigliani's nude gypsy, twenty-eight by twenty inches," Dino said.

The bidding started at $15,000, but Mubarak was quick to knock it up to $17,000. Somehow, I managed to remain quiet. I could almost see the painting in my gallery already, because the first artwork had come to me so easily.

The squealy man then bid the price to $19,000, but Mubarak increased that to $21,000.

"I will pay $23,000!" shouted fat Lorenzo, who already owned George Washington's rifle.

"No," said the squeaky Italian, shaking his head.

I increased it to $25,000, only to be outbid to $27,000 by Mubarak. Despite the price going up, I knew I had it. I just needed to wear them out, and I had some money left to bargain with.

"I'm in for $29,000," Lorenzo raised.

This is it, I said to myself at that point, because I noticed a hint of nervousness when the fat man made his bid. I then offered $45,000, still a steal for a painting of that caliber.

Dino shouted, "That's $45,000 going once...going twice..."

I saw the Italian lower his head, and I was sure it was over, but a new, vaguely familiar voice rang out from the back. "I'll give $145,000."

I turned around and was shocked to see Matthew Pearce standing by the door.

"All right, $145,000 for Mr. Pearce. Anyone want to increase?" Dino asked, seemingly just as shocked as I was.

Wearing a nasty smirk on his face, Matthew walked slowly over to me and whispered in my ear, "Now we are even, toad."

I shook my head, closed my eyes for a few seconds, took a deep breath, and calmly replied, "Even? So you are nothing more than a toad either?" Then, I stood and walked out of the room as his face reddened with fury and embarrassment and his smirk curved into a frown.

For a few days, I felt bitter about what happened in Sicily. Ivan later told me that Dino had contacted Pearce Gallery and asked if they were interested in the paintings. Straightaway, Matthew hopped on a plane to Catania, as if he knew I was going to be there and he just wanted to rub it in my face. I was lucky that his flight was a bit delayed, or I may not have even snatched Pissarro's piece.

Over the next few weeks, I kept busy planning the one-year anniversary for the gallery. I decided I would display twenty paintings from the best ten artists we had exhibited during our first year, two paintings each. I made sure to include Hakan's work. My protégé had done well for himself and had settled in Buenos Aires three months earlier, when a well-known Spanish art dealer there gave him a good offer and convinced Hakan that there was big business for his type of work. Nevertheless, Hakan gave his word that he would be there for the anniversary.

My biggest worry was finding a way to improve my permanent collection. I now had twelve paintings, with the addition of Hakan's first, which I had kept from the start. In my opinion, the one he was working on the first time I saw him was his best work. Even with that and Pissarro' work, I didn't have enough. I had a few leads on some art sales, but none of them turned out to be worthy. My concern only worsened when Professor Schmidt knocked my door on a Monday morning to tell me some news I did not want to hear.

"Pearce Gallery is holding their first exhibition in Paris on the same day as our anniversary," the professor said grimly. "They hinted that they will present paintings by Van Gogh and Picasso, some never displayed to the public before."

"That weasel! He just won't stop," I complained to Professor Schmidt.

"Don't bother yourself with thoughts of him. We will have a great show, and we have many loyal members," he replied, trying to console me.

"Yes, but I need more. I need…something," I whined.

Two days later, while Mother had her friends Madam Claudia and Madam Susanne over for dinner, I took the time to go through my finances. I could not help overhearing the women when they told Mom how proud she should be of her son, a successful businessman who was also caring and always there for her.

"His passion for art is genuine, growing by the day, unlike Captain Marcel," Madam Claudia said, referring to her young brother-in-law, who had some good art in his home but sorely neglected it. "He has paid it no attention since he fell for that Greek widow ten years younger than him. Now he's thinking of selling his place and moving to Crete with her as soon as he sorts his finances out."

I quickly put my notebook aside and joined my mother and her two dear friends. "What kind of art does he have?" I asked the old woman.

"A lot. His house is like a mini-Louvre, full of statues, maps, and paintings. I think I recall him having a Van Gogh among his ignored treasures," Madam Claudia answered.

"A Van Gogh!" I shouted at a volume that shocked everyone in the room, my mother most of all.

"Mm-hmm," she said, nodding, a bit taken aback by my excitement. "Why do you ask, Sebastian?"

"Can I meet with him next Monday?" I asked.

"I will have to ask him and get back to you."

"Please do. This might be the miracle I've been waiting for," I said, then gave her a pat on the back.

The next day, I made a few calls and met with an old colleague of mine at The Louvre. He was originally Greek, and though he had been in Paris for the past ten years, his family still lived there, in Crete, to be precise. Nikolaos was kind to meet me during his lunch break. He had been working at The Louvre for the past five years, in the accounting department. While I was employed there, our paths crossed a lot. He, like many of my previous colleagues, was a member of my gallery and visited from time to time.

"Can $40,000 buy me a villa with a swimming pool and a view of the ocean in Crete?" I asked.

"Well done, Sebastian. Your gallery must be doing real well if you are thinking of retiring early on a Greek isle," he said, clapping softly.

"No, man, I'm not asking for myself. I have a project I will tell you about later. I... Just answer my question."

"Of course it can. In fact, you may be able to do it for less. One of my cousins works in real estate," Nikolaos said.

"I like that. Just remember the swimming pool and ocean view," I repeated.

"I will call him. I'm sure he'll have something for you within a week, Sebastian."

"Speaking of family, when did you last see your parents, Nikolaos?" I asked, smiling.

"Over six months ago, Easter. Why?" he said, arching his dark brow in confusion.

"Ask The Louvre for a day off tomorrow, whatever excuse you have to make. I will book you in business class. I can't wait a full week. Come back with everything you know by Sunday night. I want pictures, damn good ones," I said.

On Sunday, as promised, I picked Nikolaos up from the airport around eight p.m., and we went straight to my gallery. The man had done his work brilliantly. *All the cards are in my hand now,* I thought, *and I only have to play them right.*

I picked up Madam Claudia at eleven a.m., as agreed, and drove to Captain Marcel's apartment in the 7th Arrondissement, a few roads behind Musée d'Orsay. She told me he was her late husband's younger brother. He was 57 and had worked as a sea captain for twenty years. On a trip seven years ago, he badly injured his knee and was forced to retire. The shipping company did not compensate him well, and he'd been in a nasty legal battle with them for a decade. He had been in a relationship with the Greek woman for fifteen years, even before her husband died. They met during one of his trips, and when her husband passed away a few years back, they could finally officially and openly be together. From what Madam Claudia told me, he was fed up with his life in Paris and just wanted to sell everything and move away with the woman he loved, to get a fresh start after a lot of rough turns in life.

Captain Marcel lived in a small, one-bedroom apartment on the fourth floor of nice building built after World War II, and he welcomed us politely when we arrived. He was slightly overweight but dressed nicely in black trousers, a blue and white striped shirt, and a hat on his bald head.

His living room was dimly lit. The floors were wooden, and the furniture was brown, and it felt like being in a very small maritime museum. The house was full of model ships and ship wheels. There were also many strange statues that appeared to be African; I guessed they were souvenirs from his trips abroad. Then I saw it, the collectible I'd come for, an oil painting of a pot of sunflowers next to a window. I had no doubt that it was a genuine Van Gogh, and my eyes sparkled with delight when I saw it. On a shelf on the other side of the room was a self-portrait of Frida Kahlo, arguably the greatest Mexican artist that had ever lived. "I need them," I said to myself while smiling at the captain.

"I am sorry my place isn't so tidy," he apologized as he opened the curtains to a perfect view of the Eiffel Tower. "I have heard a lot of good things about you, Sebastian. You are often mentioned at the café I go to in Montmartre. People talk of your gallery in Le Marias, say you have helped many young artists get a start," he continued as we all sat down on his leather chairs.

"Thank you, Captain. I am just opening the path for art," I replied shyly.

"So, Claudia, to what do I owe this visit? I hope you are not trying to convince me to change my decision like you have been for the past months, dragging this young, reputed man into our drama. No matter what you say, I am going to Crete. I must free myself from this small box."

"I agree with you, Captain. The sea and the weather are beautiful in Greece, but look at your view of Paris! It is a shame that you have to sell this place," I said as I opened my briefcase and took out three files to place in front of him.

Curiously, the captain opened the files and pulled the photographs out. "What is this?" he asked, looking closely at one.

"You can own any of those villas within forty-eight hours, Captain, and you do not even have to sell this apartment."

"How?" he asked, looking at me with great skepticism in his eyes.

"I merely want those two paintings and that statue, in exchange for a fifteen-year lease with an obligation to buy them all for $1,500,000 in 1994."

The captain and his sister-in-law looked at me in shock but said nothing.

"Of course, this one must be properly authenticated," I said, moving closer to the Van Gogh.

"Did you say $1,500,000?" Madam Claudia asked, astonished.

"You have a view of the Eiffel Tower here. Don't sell. My friend's cousin is a violinist, now with The Orchestre de Chambre, the new orchestra in Paris. She would be happy to rent this place. She is a wonderful lady and will take good care of it. You will also have a Convertible Volkswagen Beetle, 1977, and a small fishing boat," I said as I moved towards Frida Kahlo's work.

"Authenticated? Of course they are real," the captain said. "That Van Gogh painting was my father's gift to me when I joined the navy, back before World War I. I bought Frida's back in 1957, when I was on an assignment there. That naked boy sculpture by Constantin Brâncuşi was a gift to my father from the sculptor himself. Hmm. I've never really thought of how valuable they are. Maybe I should sell them. Why wait?" the captain replied with confidence.

"I am sure you would get a good price, around $700,000 or $800,000 within six months, maybe a year. Authentication is a long process, and then there is registration and... Well, it is a lot of red tape really. If you have that kind of time, I suppose you could go through the normal procedure," I said as I closed the curtains, trying to remind him of the dim environment he lived in.

The man looked around his place. "But you say I can have the villa, the car, and boat now, then $1,500,000? I'll be 72 by then, not a young man. Who knows if I will even be living. Hmm. If I die, you will pay it to whomever I say, correct?" the captain asked as he continued thumbing through the photos.

"Forty-eight hours, Captain, and on January 2, 1994, a payment of $1,500,000 will be made to whomever you please."

"This one," the captain said, handing the second folder to me.

"Then it's a deal," I said with a smile that matched his.

I left the place with the two paintings in hand. The car, and boat offers just came out of nowhere, but it still fell well within my budget. The villa the captain chose was $34,500, and the Beetle, and boat would be about $5,500. I gained those precious pieces for less than $40,000, and in 15 years, those and the statue would be worth multiple times what I put up for offer in the first place.

As soon as I got home. I told my mother to call the insurance company and set up a meeting the first thing the next morning. I needed to insure my new beauties with a nice policy, and I knew it was going to be costly. I wasn't worried about that, though, because I could lease the statue to other galleries and museums, and the insurance would be paid in no time.

"Two Exhibitions, One Day. Mark Your Calendars."

"Paris Is Art."

"Pearce or Allure Gallerie?"

The headlines went on and on, and the whole town was talking about the two upcoming art shows. For our part, ten artists would be sharing twenty paintings to throngs of visitors, and champagne, wine, and food would be served.

The anniversary was a success. Jannette played beautifully in the main gallery, dressed in a long white gown. My permanent collection, now consisting of fourteen paintings, was a thing of beauty for the world to see.

For six continuous hours, the place was packed. Akram Shukri and Mrs. Stanley were absent due to health issues, and Ana couldn't be there because she had a show of her own in Chicago that day. Still, she managed to find time to call three times to find out how things were going.

Ultimately, there wasn't really a winner or loser in the rivalry between Pearce and Allure Gallerie. Pearce Gallery had lovely paintings to show, but my Allure Gallerie offered a mix of youth and history, enough to go toe to toe with them. Pearce's plan to ruin the day for us did not succeed, and he was none too happy that we were just getting more powerful.

The true winners were the art-loving Parisians, who got to see art at their doorsteps, and I couldn't have been happier about that.

Chapter Seven

In the four years that followed, it seemed most of my life and work revolved around that sneaky Englishman Matthew Pearce and his ongoing ploys against the gallery. In reality, they were personal attacks against me. To protect my business, I had to follow his every move, to keep up on all the latest gossip about him, and he did the same when it came to me. It seemed every conversation I had begun and ended was related with that man and our numerous battles, often face-to-face confrontations at auctions. I managed to score a few paintings, but my adversary usually ended up on top. Twice, he sent men from London, and they offered to buy my business for any figure I had in mind, but I refused to give in to his greed. I knew he would only close my beloved gallery, and all my hopes and dreams would end with that sort of hostile takeover.

Like some battle-worn general in a never-ending war, I was constantly obsessed with thoughts of my enemy: *What's new with Matthew? What has he bought now? Where is he headed next?* That went on for a long time, until life smacked me with a distracting reality check with a call from afar.

"Hello, Sebastian. Is that you?" asked a familiar voice.

"Yes. This is Sebastian. Who is speaking?" I replied.

"This is Frank, Frank Schull."

"From Miami?" I asked, shocked to hear from him. Ana had mentioned him several times over the years, since she saw him at exhibitions a number of times, but I hadn't even spoken to the man for almost six years, since the night he booked my flight back to Paris when we found out about my mother's stroke. "Mr. Schull, it's good to hear from you? How are you?"

"I should be asking you of that, more so about your dear mother. How is she?"

"Well, I'm glad to say. But what can I do for you, Frank?"

"Well, I'm sorry to bother you at this time, but I'm not sure if you've heard…" He trailed off, as if something was very wrong.

"Heard what, Frank?" I anxiously inquired, not at all liking the worrisome tone in his voice.

"Well, I'm not quite sure how to put it into words. It's Ana. She's had…an accident."

"What!? What are you talking about? What accident? I talked to her only a week ago, and she was fine. Is she all right? Where is she, and why didn't anyone call me sooner?" I shouted, my heart beating rapidly in my chest as I imagined the worst about my sweet Ana.

170

"I'm trying to tell you now, Sebastian. I guess it happened two days ago. I just got here yesterday morning. I was furious with her agent, Monica, when I learned that no one had notified you. I know how much she meant to you."

Meant? As in...past tense? Is she gone? my mind screamed, but I didn't dare interrupt, because I needed all the details.

"One of the plane engines blew while she was attempting to land. She crashed in a forest. Luckily, the impact wasn't fatal, but..." Again, he hesitated.

"But what? Speak up, Frank!" I demanded. I could feel the nervous sweat running down my whole body.

"Ana was in a coma, but she awoke ten hours ago. She suffered third-degree burns on her hand and second-degree ones from her elbow to her shoulder. The surgeons had to do an operation on her thumb and index finger because of the burns, and—"

"Which hand?" I interrupted.

"I am afraid the damage was done to her right one," Frank said, trying to hide a sniffle of his own.

"Oh no," I muttered, closing my eyes as soon as I heard it.

"There is something else, Sebastian," he continued. "Her vitals are good, but she seems to be suffering from amnesia, doesn't know where or who she is. She will only speak in French, not a word of English. The doctors say it's probably the result of a severe concussion."

No longer could I hold back my tears, and I felt them roll down my cheeks, hot and salty. "Wh-Where is she now?" I managed, albeit barely audibly.

"Jackson Memorial Hospital, getting the best treatment possible. She was supposed to attend a show tonight in Miami, but... Anyway, I'm sorry to be the bearer of bad news, but I called as soon as I found out."

"I will take the first flight out," I said, all thoughts of Matthew Pearce instantly forgotten. "Thank you for calling, Frank," I said.

As soon as I hung up the phone, it rang again.

"Sebastian, do you know?" Émilie said, crying hysterically.

"Yes," I said, but I could not utter another word.

"Is she...dead? Please tell me she isn't! I heard about the Florida plane crash on the news, but they didn't give too many details. They only said 'The artist is in critical condition,'" she said, crying and moaning between every syllable.

"Thankfully, she's still with us, Émilie. She's lost some things, just not her life," I explained sadly. "Please try to remain calm. Dear Ana wouldn't want us to be so upset. I'll be at your place within the hour," I said.

As soon as I put the phone down, I hurried to the door and turned the sign around to let everyone know the gallery was closed. I turned off all the lights except the spotlight in the main room, where Ana's work was illuminated. I stared at it for a moment, sobbing even worse than my friend was on the phone.

After I practiced what I preached and calmed down a bit, I made several calls and booked the earliest flight to Miami I could, departing the next morning. For the first time in years, I totally forgot that I even had an enemy in the art business.

At home, I told my mother about the incident, and she insisted on dressing and going with me to Antoine and Émilie's place. I filled them in on everything Frank had told me. I then made the difficult call to Ana's sister to tell her what I knew and to let her know I was going to Ana in the morning.

Patrice, who had been working with us for the past six months, offered to fill in for me during what I assumed would be an extended absence. I was very fond of the young man, who was one of the first members to join our gallery. He came to every exhibition we held, and he knew so much about art and the pieces we displayed.

Patrice visited me the day after he graduated from the University of Sorbonne, with a degree in art history. He told me of his desire to work at the gallery. I loved his passion, so I offered him a job right away. He was particularly interested in the impressionist era. He could talk for hours about each artist, and he got along well with all of my staff, so he was a great addition to our team. He had even helped me find some auctions I wouldn't have otherwise known about. He was the reason I got my hands on Giovanni Segantini's *Mountain of Hope* landscape painting from a private dealer for a tenth of its price. To many in the art industry this was the catch of the last decade.

Since my mother was getting older and I was very busy at the gallery, Mrs. André had been taking care of Mother more often. Nevertheless, mother showed up at the gallery twice a week, the days when Professor Schmidt was there, and the two of them enjoyed one another's company. Now, it was good to know that Mrs. André would be there to faithfully look after my mom while I had to be away.

"Stay strong, Sebastian. Bring Ana back. She is the spark in your life," my mother said, then gave me a kiss and a tight hug.

I left just as dawn broke. As I sat in the window seat on my flight to the States, I stared out at the wing, thinking of all the horror Ana must have gone through when she knew her flight was doomed.

She'd been taking flying lessons for the past two years. "I find great solace in flying, Sebastian, great peace," she told me when I asked her about it. "In the air, I can leave the world behind, just forget about everything down here. It's as if I can leave all my stress on the ground far below."

Over the years, we'd met mostly in London, since her work was in high demand there. She only came back to France a few times, and we could only spend a few days together before we had to return to our normal lives. As always, we confided in one another about everything, as often as we could.

Of course, that wasn't often enough for either of us, with all the miles and an ocean between us. Just a week before her crash, Ana had mentioned to me that she was thinking of returning to Paris for good. She had made lots of money, and she just wanted to be a free spirit again. Her work had become "too mechanical," as she put it, "too forced," and she no longer felt it portrayed her inner feelings. We had even started giving some thought to spending our lives together, but that was all before the horrible accident intervened and threatened to spoil those plans.

As soon as I reached the hospital, I asked to see the surgeon in charge. He gently explained the precariousness of her situation to me. Then, after a few hours, he allowed me to visit her in the sterile, isolated room where she was resting. The nurses ordered me to dress in a special gown, with disposable covers for my feet, face, and hair, because she was very susceptible to infections at that time.

I found Ana staring at the window, blank and expressionless, in the brightly lit room, with her right arm wrapped in bandages and suspended above her thin waist. For a moment, I could only stand there and stare at her in terrified awe. "Bonjour, Ana," I finally said, keeping my distance as I tried to gather my composure.

"Bonjour, monsieur," she replied faintly, like a scared little girl speaking to a stranger.

I could not resist taking a few steps back and removing my hood and facemask, desperately hoping she'd recognize me. "How are you?" I said, speaking in our mother tongue.

She instantly found her beautiful smile again, that smile I saw in my dreams so many times, and her gorgeous eyes and face lit up. "I am not sure I know you, sir, yet I feel as if a big burden has just been lifted from my chest," she replied as she raised her left arm to greet me.

I looked at the nurse, and she motioned for me to put the mask back on before I approached sweet Ana. "You *do* know me, perhaps better than anyone, and I know you as well. I am Sebastian," I softly said.

Ana smiled again, looking me in the eyes. Then she covered herself with the sheets and closed her eyes.

"My Red Queen," I said as she drifted off to sleep.

In the days that followed, I tried not to bombard Ana with too many details. I just explained that we were good friends in Paris. The medical team helped me cope with her condition and informed me of what steps I could take to help her, since I was very close to her.

"We are facing three situations," the doctor said. "First, she must fully recover from her serious burns. Second, she will have to come to terms with the loss of her digits."

I had never been too squeamish of a person, but I shuddered as they tried to enlighten me as to the reasons behind the necessity of amputating her thumb and finger. "By the time Ana reached the hospital, she was bleeding profusely from her right hand, particularly from those two fingers, which were injured by shards of glass, plastic, and metal from the crash. The nerve damage was irreversible," the surgeon said. "It was a difficult decision, especially considering her career, but the risk of infection was too high. She could have lost her entire arm down the road if we did not make that smaller sacrifice."

"And what is the third predicament, Doctor?" I asked.

"Well, she is dealing with severe memory loss, as you know, Sebastian. That will take a great deal to improve, possibly longer than her physical recovery."

The medical staff informed me that her burns could take up to three weeks to heal. Ana had to be kept on IV fluids for the duration, and she would be treated with daily doses of potent antibiotics. Her bandages had to be changed daily as well, with ointment applied to prevent any blisters or infection.

"I know all of this sounds awful, but I assure you she is in the best of hands here," one of the nurses said. "It will be only a matter of time before she is better."

As for the loss of her fingers, they looked at it from a physical point of view as well as a mental and emotional one. They expected that the pain and swelling would ease within two to three weeks, and with proper physiotherapy and painkillers, the pain and soreness would gradually cease. "She may want to consider plastic surgery for aesthetic reasons, but it is too early to tell if that is an option," the doctor said, handing me a pile of brochures about the available procedures and artificial attachments. "There may also be prosthetics she can use in place of her lost fingers. As for her emotional wellbeing, you need to be aware that your friend may suffer some depression and a feeling of uselessness. All patients differ, Sebastian, and some adapt faster than others. There have been many advancements in prosthetics, and we are optimistic that science will lend a helping hand to ease Ana's distress and improve her functioning after this loss."

I understood the importance of therapy and aftercare, considering what I'd been through with my mother. "I will do my best to find good follow-up care back in Paris, for her mental and physical wellbeing," I assured them.

"You are an excellent, caring friend, Sebastian. She is blessed to have that kind of support, and it will aid in her recovery," the doctor said.

As for the memory loss, the medical team was rather straightforward with her prognosis; they could not say if it would be temporary or permanent. The tests they ran in the first eight days showed no serious brain or head injury, apart from the bruise on the right side of her head. They could only surmise that her concussion was more serious than they originally thought.

"Have patience with our patient, my friend," the nurse told me. "Just be natural when you talk to her, and don't push her too hard."

I was very gentle and patient with Ana, but was also by her side every minute I could be. For the first month, I slept at the hospital every night, but I could only see her once a day, unless Ana called and requested a visit. She began to ask for me more often, and we talked a lot about the nature of my work. It was like meeting her all over again. We laughed about things as we went on small walks through the hospital corridors, and we enjoyed watching movies I rented, all in French, of course.

I also met Monica, Ana's agent and attorney. I wasn't that surprised when she informed me that Ana had listed me as her beneficiary, in case anything ever happened to her. Truth be told, she was much closer to me than to anyone else, no matter the distance between us.

"Because Ana is incapacitated by her memory loss, she has been declared mentally unfit. You will be in charge of her financial affairs until the hospital deems that her medical condition has improved," Monica told me, handing me a stack of forms, files, and paperwork. "If you have any questions, do let me know."

Ana's bank account was quite hefty, carrying a balance of over $200,000. The money from the exhibition she missed had not been deposited yet, but Frank informed me that all twelve of her paintings sold almost instantly, at the highest price, so I could expect another $45,000 to be transferred to her soon. "That happens sometimes, traumatic events making one's work more valuable," he said.

When I told Ana about her financial situation and the fact that I'd been asked to handle it, she said, "Hmm. Well, if I signed that power over to you, then that's that. I realize money is important, but I just don't remember what for. I don't even know what costs what, so it's probably best for you to deal with it for now," she said, rather dismissively.

I called Paris and was told that everything at home was fine. I was pleased to hear that Mother was doing so well. "Mrs. André comes with the sun, early in the morning, and she doesn't leave till I'm snug in bed in the evenings," she assure me.

Thanks to Patrice, the gallery was moving along smoothly as well. When he warned me that Matthew Pearce had sent the same pushy potential buyers, I couldn't have cared less. "They know you're in Miami," he said. "I told them you're dealing with a very important personal matter and they ought to leave you alone."

"Don't worry about those dogs," I said. "Let them bark all they will. I'm not going to throw them a bone!"

When I spoke to Émilie, I asked her to try to find a nice, small place for Ana to stay, close to where I lived. A few days later, she contacted me to let me know she'd discovered a cozy loft. "Furnish it comfortably and decorate it with bright colors," I instructed. "Make sure to use light window coverings, so we can let plenty of that Paris sunshine in."

"I've never known Ana to have an inclination for bright places," Émilie said.

"Well, she does now. Maybe it's all this hospital white," I said.

I also talked with Ana's closest sister. I told her we would be back in four days, on a Tuesday, and I planned to invite them all to the gallery for lunch on Sunday.

That Monday night, the medical team met with Ana and me, and we had a long talk about her case. Both of us understood exactly what was needed.

"Are you sure you are prepared to leave the hospital, Ana?" asked Dr. Stevens, the physician who'd been in charge of taking care with her. "Paris is rather far away, and you are just getting to know your friend again."

"Yes, Doctor," she said, never taking her eyes off of me. Then she whispered, "I trust you, Sebastian."

"That is all I want from you Ana, trust," I whispered back.

Antoine and Émilie picked us up from the airport. After the introductions were made, we ate a quick dinner together and called it a night. Émilie was happy that

Ana loved her new home. It was especially nice because it was only a few streets away from my place.

The next day, we visited one of the medical centers that was recommended to us back in the States. Ana underwent a full checkup, and a cast was taken of her hand so they could create custom-tailored prosthetics to help her. "You'll need to come in for weekly checkups, Ana," the doctor there told us.

For the next two days, I took her on tours of Paris, reintroducing her to the city. I remembered what the nurse told me in Miami, and I didn't pummel her with too many details about her former life. I only answered her general questions about her past, like where she had lived and what restaurants she used to enjoy dining in. Whenever I felt a temptation to mention some specific detail or event that might be difficult for her to ponder, I remembered Dr. Stevens's wise words: "Patience with the patient, Sebastian."

When Ana visited my gallery, she enjoyed looking at all the paintings.

"That's the one you created," I said.

To my surprise, she giggled.

"That girl was an excellent painter," I said, laughing back, though the words stung a bit.

I made sure to clearly elaborate on Ana's real condition to her family before they showed up for lunch. I also told them what the doctors advised about taking it easy and give her some space. We will only introduce each of you to her, then follow Ana's lead," I said. "Please try to refrain from showing too much emotion, especially anything that will be...demotivating."

Soon, Ana's family arrived, along with my mother, Professor Schmidt, Antoine, Émilie, and their daughter. Madam Marianne, who had handled all my catering since my grand opening so many years ago, prepared a nice luncheon in the front area of the gallery, plenty of duck breast, steak, and merlot or chardonnay for twelve guests. Of course, Madam Marianne asked her chef to prepare a special plate of chicken for the picky professor.

The lunch went better than I expected. Ana's family did an amazing job of hiding their sadness, but I could feel it, as I'd been going through the same emotions myself for over a month. It was a painful experience to care about someone who didn't even know who I was, but it was our unfortunate reality, at least for the time being. We could only hope that things would change for the better.

As the months went by, Ana visited the gallery a few times a week. She loved to see the new work on display, and her natural eye for good art was still evident. Sometimes, she stared at the paintings for a while, then shared her thoughts with the artists. At times, we went out for drinks. Sometimes, it was just the two of us, and other times, we invited Émilie. Ana enjoyed her company very much, just as she had in the past. She also enjoyed jogging, so much that she made the healthy habit part of her daily routine. From time to time, she visited other museums; of them, The Louvre was her favorite. She seemed happy with her prosthesis and adapted to it well. Before long, she began to show signs of her old self, the same lively soul who loved to joke and laugh. She was the same crazy Ana I always knew, only lacking so many of the precious memories I'd hoped we'd both cherish forever.

I called Dr. Stevens several times to discuss her condition. "You may have to accept the fact that she might never get her memory back, Sebastian," he said, as gently as he could. "Perhaps it is time for her to start a new life."

As happy as I was that Ana seemed content in moving forward as she was now, I still felt she had a right to know about her past. *She deserves that*, I thought. *I only have to figure out the best time to tell her.* Then, one day, it came to me, and I knew exactly what I had to do.

On a Saturday night, I took Ana to see a movie at the cinema in Le Marais, during a week when they were playing classic films. I could think of nothing better for us to see than *Casablanca*, because those scenes with Hollywood legends Humphrey Bogart and Ingrid Bergman were so full of passion. Despite having seen the movie twice before, I was touched by it once again, and Ana even cried at the end. As I walked her home, I knew the time had come for me to finally tell her what was inside me all long.

"What did you think of the movie?" I asked.

"She should have stayed with him," she replied sadly.

"Didn't you feel you were part of that story, like you're...living it?"

"Yes, I suppose, but why do you ask?" she said, her face etched with confusion.

"I don't know. Do you think you'll remember *Casablanca* four years from now, even a decade later?"

"Yes, forever," she said, with not a shred of doubt in her voice. "Why are you asking me these questions, Sebastian?"

"Wouldn't you love to see your *own* movie, to really live it, Ana?" I said as I placed my hands on her slender shoulders and looked her straight in the eyes.

"Yes, I would," she replied, with tears flooding into her green eyes.

"Come on then."

I led her to the gallery, where I dimmed all the lights except for the small table lamp in my office. I opened a bottle of wine and talked nonstop to her, for the next four hours. While showing her snapshots of herself and her family, I told her what I knew about her childhood. I was so glad her sister had kindly offered me the photos a few days earlier, when the idea came to me and I shared it with her.

Eventually, her life story led to the chapter when we met. I told Ana about our first interaction at the lecture, our endless nights at the seine, about my guitar, the jazz, the dancing, her paintings, her colors, the rainy nights, her loud laughs with Émilie, our first night in Miami, the swimming pool, London, the opening night at our gallery, our passionate nights, our first kiss, and the evening we made love in the car. I even laughed about the time she turned me into a red man. "We deeply cared about each other, Ana," I said, taking her hand. "We both loved our work, too, though, and we never pressured one another in our relationship. We never fought, and we always understood one another's needs." I then opened the drawer and showed her more pictures and some articles, write-ups and praises about her and her work in dozens of magazines, from her exhibitions in galleries all over the world. "This is your *Casablanca*, Ana. These are your characters and props and plots and actors, and I suppose I am your—"

She moved close to me and put a finger against my lips to shush me. "Sebastian, when you first walked into my hospital room and took off that silly mask and hood, I felt my heart beat faster than ever before. All this time, I've been afraid to say anything, terrified that you were just a close friend to me and nothing more, like a brother. I have loved you willingly and unwillingly ever since that moment."

"And I loved you since our eyes first met in Professor's Schmidt lecture back then. When you said yes a few hours ago, I fell in love with you all over again."

She looked at me and kissed me wildly, and that night, we made love till dawn, just as passionately as before.

After a while, Ana showed her desire to work at the gallery. I was very happy that the request came from her, as her energy was exactly what we were lacking. Since her accident, I'd not been as involved with my gallery, and while business was stable, the momentum suffered a bit. Now, we had something new and exciting to look forward to again.

Professor Schmidt loved being around women, and Ana and my mother were great company for him, so he started coming to work every day of the week. With his insight, Patrice's vast knowledge, Ana's art, and my newly piqued interest, the wheel started to turn fast again. We all knew art was no longer constrained majorly to Europe; there was so much talent in the world, and we had to go out and fish for it. So, we set our sights on a new target: Central and South America.

We laid out a detailed action plan. Then, after making several calls and inquiries, Patrice brushed up on his Spanish and traveled for a month in Brazil, Argentina, Mexico, and Colombia. There, he met with students from a number of art colleges, as well as street artists. He checked out the hipster scene, where the contemporary art movement was thriving. His fair command of the language was a big help to him, and he returned with videocassette recordings of interviews of many artists, as well as photographs he had taken of paintings and of the artists themselves.

From the thirty-nine artists Patrice discovered on his trip, we selected only four to have a place in our gallery. We agreed to pay for their travel expenses and accommodations, as well as to let them keep 50 percent of their sales. Each would be granted one week to exhibit in our first-ever Latino month at the Allure Gallerie in Le Marais.

I invited a Mexican mariachi band to play during the opening ceremony each week. While they sang and played their festive tunes, sparkling wine and tequila was served. We hung colorful lamps from the ceilings.

At auction, I also managed to snatch another Frida Kahlo painting, at a fair price. As soon as Roberto, our Italian host, said "Sold, to Signor Sebastian!" I nearly jumped out of my seat. The new addition would be presented for the first time in the second week of our Latino art celebration. Off course, that purchase did not go over well with Matthew Pearce, who was quite taken by surprise by our sudden resurgence.

At the end of Latino month, not a single painting was left. Everything sold, sixty pieces in all, and it proved to be our most successful endeavor yet. It was the first exhibition Ana and I did together, and we enjoyed every minute of it. It was her idea to spice things up with the colorful lamps and the tequila, and it paid off.

Outside of work, we were on the seventh cloud. We jogged and biked together, all over Paris. We tried new recipes, cooking weird food from all over the world, in her kitchen and mine. When I proposed two months later, she didn't hesitate to say yes, and we were happily married later that year at Notre Dame. We were sad to leave our friends after such a wonderful day, but we were very excited to travel to Egypt, then Kenya, for our ten-day honeymoon.

Our first stop was Cairo, and we spent a few days there. Ana and I loved the hospitality and generosity of the Egyptian people, as well as their unforgettable food and colorful markets. Hand in hand, we roamed around Khan el-Khalili market, Souk, as it was called in Arabic. In the tenth century, during the Fatimid Caliphate era, it was a mausoleum site. After the fall of those leaders, the Souk gradually transformed into a trading hub, with vendors offering everything from spices and food to garments and home goods. Ana was not too shy to try on one scarf after another, and every color revealed a new layer of her beauty. When we tired of shopping hours later, we wandered through the narrow streets till the late hours, occasionally stopping at the cafés and restaurants for a bite.

We also enjoyed riding camels during our visit to Al Giza, the site of the Great Pyramids and the Sphinx, true wonders of the world. We then relaxed for several days as we cruised between Aswan and Luxor, taking in the scenery along the route of the Nile, especially as we passed through impressive ancient Egyptian temples. "It's unbelievable that they built such enormous, detailed structures, all by hand," Ana said. We had both seen some fragments off Egyptian history at The Louvre, but being there, in direct contact with the origin of it, was an experience all its own.

Our next stop was Nairobi, in Kenya. From there, we made our way to the Maasai Mara National Reserve, were we had booked a tent for four days. Ana and I both felt we'd journeyed into another world, one humankind had never interfered with. It was Earth in its purest, most raw, most natural form. The forests, deserts, trees, and rivers appeared untouched, and wildlife roamed freely about. We spent days following the great migration of the wildebeests, gazelles, and zebras. At night, we sat down by the fire pit at our campground and gazed up at the star-filled skies, listening to the chirps, caws, and rustling of the animals and insects lurking nearby. We said nothing, as there were no words that needed to be said; the looks in our eyes and the warmth of our kisses said enough. Being so immersed in nature for the first time in our lives was overwhelming for us both. It had been an eventful year, in good and bad ways, and that trip just melted all our stress away.

Four nights later, we were on our way back to Nairobi when John, our driver, said he needed to make an urgent stop in one of the small villages near Narok. There was some sort off engine problem with our Jeep, because smoke started billowing out from under the hood. The old mechanic took a good look at the vehicle and determined, "Leak in radiator, small hole in this hose." He then told John, "Can fix in a few hours."

Since we had some unexpected free time on our hands, we decided to take a gander at one of the local markets, to see what the village had to offer. Most of the small stalls or kiosks were managed by young mothers or girls taking care of babies. Many laid their items out on cloth on the ground, and they were happy to sell whatever they had, from jewelry made of stones to wooden statues similar to those I'd seen in Captain Marcel's humble home some years back. We saw no young men around; there were only a few elderly, wrinkled males wandering here and there, and that seemed rather strange to us. *Where did these babies come from then?* I had to wonder.

While Ana knelt down to play with one of the infants, a tall, young mother with big, brown eyes waved a piece of paper around and said something to her in Swahili.

"What did she say?" Ana asked John, as she was unfamiliar with that dialect.

"She wants to draw Ana's eye," our driver replied.

"My eye? Hmm. Go ahead," Ana said, then sat down beside the woman and crossed her legs.

The girl looked at Ana a few times, then began applying charcoal to the paper in her hand. Twenty minutes later, she smiled shyly and showed her drawing to us. There was something so pure and innocent about her face, and her grin was simply irresistible. Even more amazing was her work; Ana's eye was perfectly replicated in the middle of the paper, and there appeared to be a story reflected within it.

Ana and I looked at each other in awe. Over the years, I'd seen many portraits drawn, but I'd never seen such a detailed eye before, and certainly none had ever captured such a story with just a chunk of charcoal.

"John, ask her about it," I requested.

He nodded, and after the two talked a bit, he looked at us and scrunched up his brow. "I-I'm not sure how to say this," he said.

"Just tell us what she said," I encouraged.

"She said there are two women in Madam Ana's eyes, not one."

"Did she really say that?" Ana asked, looking at me.

"Yes, something like that."

I pointed at the young lady and gestured for her to draw me.

She smiled again and motioned for me to sit down.

"Sir Sebastian, we don't have much time. We need to pick up the Jeep soon, so we can get to the airport in time for your flight," John interrupted.

I looked at my watch. "We'll be fine. She does quick work," I said, then smiled and sat quietly next to her.

Twenty minutes later, she held up a new drawing for us to examine. As much as I loved the uniqueness in it, it was the story she'd captured that really caught my interest. There, on that paper, was an image of a figure, apparently chasing something.

When the artist saw me staring at it, she leaned over and said something to John.

"Revenge," John said. "She says she sees vengeance in you."

"Matthew," Ana said, looking at me.

I quickly pulled my wallet out of my small bag, removed my two remaining $100 bills, and gave it to the young woman. "For both," I said, taking the two drawings from her. "Ana, Sebastian," I introduced, pointing at myself and Ana in turn.

"Layla," she said shyly, still wearing her adorable smile.

I asked Ana for the camera she was carrying, then turned my attention back to the young woman. "May I take a photo of you, Layla?" I said, holding the gadget up and hoping she'd understand.

Clearly no stranger to tourists with photography equipment, Layla nodded, and her smile broadened.

I took several photos of her, her drawings, and her baby. Then, I asked John to take a photo of all of us together. "John, please tell her I will be in touch," I said. "I will need you to gather as much information about her as you can. I want to know...anything and everything she'll share about herself and her life.

Before we left, Ana and I waved goodbye to the talented mother, then took several more photos of the village fate had led us to.

On the way back to the airport in Nairobi, we learned more about the misfortune of people in Nafok and most of Africa. "The harsh reality is that many are widowed at a young age, when their men are killed by the militia. Some men have to travel far from their wives and children to work in faraway places, sometimes for days or weeks at a time. Sometimes, the menfolk just flee, feeling too burdened by the difficult responsibilities of fatherhood, leaving the mothers with nothing. That $200 you gave to Layla may be more than she's made in the last year." We also learned that marriage at a very young age was common, while education was rare, and there was almost a 100 percent illiteracy rate in most villages.

On the flight back, Ana and I had much to talk about. Mostly, we shared our feelings about poor Layla and the women like her, and we vowed to make a change in that part of the world if we could.

The moment we returned to Paris, I called my dear friend Antoine and invited him over to my place.

"Are you sure? I don't want to bother the newlyweds," he teased.

"It's rather urgent," I said, then went on to tell him what we'd discovered in that village so far away during our honeymoon. "It's awful, Antoine, all those young mothers going through poverty. Layla was...as beautiful as her work. She and the others deserve better lives."

When Antoine arrived we showed him the drawings and the photographs we'd captured with our Kodak.

"We must do something soon," I said. "We all know third-world countries suffer from poverty and illiteracy, but Layla's story... Well, hopefully, something good will come out of our honeymoon visit, besides the happy memories we made with each other," I said, holding my wife's hand.

"I think I can help, at least a little. I'll write an article and submit it everywhere. Hopefully, it will be published on many front pages. Sharing stories is what I do. Leave that to me," he said, looking at the photo of Layla holding that paper in her hand, smiling with her toddler next to her.

Three newspapers published Antoine's article, and within a week, everyone around Paris seemed to be talking about Layla and the women of Africa. It was the topic of all the chitchat in the streets and in the cafés, as well as on TV and radio. Before we knew it, Ana and I were even invited to be interviewed for a program. My spouse was great on camera, and she practically glowed as she answered the questions. Ana just took over, and she was so articulate and confident that I let her go on and on.

"Crazy Ana, my Red Queen," I said to myself.

The host of the program shed a few tears during the recording, especially when Ana shared our photos of the village, of Layla's child, and of the run-down market stalls.

When I was able to get a couple off words in edgewise, I made sure to brag about the artistic talent of the young mother. "Not only can Layla draw eyes to perfection, but she can also read them, find stories in them. She does it all with a smile on her face, despite the difficulties her and millions of others face there every day," I said.

Before the end of the show, I managed to throw in a public plea, a request for the French government to issue Layla and her child a visa so she could display her work at our gallery. All the money generated from the exhibition would go to Layla and her community.

"Schools. They need education. Knowledge is power," Ana said to end the program.

The French embassy, after catching wind of the story, made many contacts with the authorities in Nairobi. With John's help, Layla and her child were located, and she was issued a passport and visa for both of them.

We were back in Kenya within a fortnight. When we landed there, we met with many government officials, as well as some humanitarians from various organizations, to discuss how situations could be improved.

Two days later, we arrived at Charles de Gaulle airport, where we were greeted by a pack of reporters. Layla and her child were by our side as we were all bombarded with questions. Our eyes blurred as camera after camera flashed, catching snapshots of us all as we made our way to the waiting cab.

"I will make an official statement by tomorrow afternoon!" I yelled to the crowd before I climbed in.

Ana's old flat was still there, and the rent was paid till December, just over a month to go. Layla and her child would be comfortable there, and we agreed that it was best that Ana stayed with them, since they were new to Paris and the modern world. Just as it was for us in Africa, it was a whole new world for our visitors, an entirely different life than the one Layla flew away from.

Ana was very intelligent, and the plane crash, coma, and concussion did not take that from her. As soon as we returned from our honeymoon in Kenya, she began studying Swahili. She attended three classes a week at one of the eastern African centers in Paris. She also spent several hours reading on her own, at the gallery and at home, in preparation for Layla's visit.

Not only that, but my wonderful wife also thoughtfully filled the refrigerator at her former residence with food and drinks of all sorts, and she even bought a few toys for the child. She did her best to make their stay as pleasant as possible. When I dropped them off and spent a little time with them, I could see that the mother and child were happy, but my Ana was even happier that she'd done something nice for them, to give them a warm, loving welcome to our city.

The next morning, we all went to the gallery, where we were joined by Professor Schmidt and Patrice. We laid out the plan for the important exhibition, then worked together on the statement that would be passed on to press through Antoine, who had joined us with a cameraman. As the day went by and news of Layla's presence in Paris started to spread, many people showed up at the gallery to meet her and to offer any help they could.

While she was clearly flattered, the young mother was also visibly overwhelmed. She did not understand the impact she had made. After a while, Ana thought it was best to give her a break, and she took the girl and her baby away. I asked the people to respect her privacy but assured them that everyone would eventually have a chance to show their kindness.

The next morning, the papers published all the details about our upcoming event, a ten-day exhibition we called "Layla's Eye." We planned to put twenty of Layla's drawings on display, and we would sell them for $1,000 each. All of them would be drawings of eyes, her expression of random Parisians living their normal daily lives. "Layla will come to you," I told all the people who asked. "She has an eye for eyes!"

The idea came to us that very morning, and we decided that Layla would be escorted around Paris by Ana. They would visit random places like cafés, schools, and parks, at all hours of the day and night. There, with permission, Layla would draw the eyes of the people she met, and those drawings would form the collection for our exhibit.

At the same time, during the exhibition, Layla would create five new drawings daily, for a fee of $2,500 each, a total of fifty new drawings over the ten days. Twenty-five of the lucky candidates would be pulled from a lottery of interested gallery members, and the other twenty-five would be selected from those who registered by phone. All income from the event would be sent to organizations that promised to build suitable schools in Kenya, under Ana's and Layla's supervision.

Our two phones would not stop ringing, from early morning till evening, and over 4,000 hopefuls signed up for a chance. They included people from all walks of life, such as businessmen, politicians, doctors, actors, soccer players, and common folk. The selections were announced in the newspapers two days prior to the beginning of the event.

The whole thing became national news in no time, and praise poured in from cities all over the world. Everyone sent their regards and offered to help, save one person.

My nemesis, Matthew Pearce, also used word-of-mouth, but he did so in a negative way, to slander and insult. A reporter asked for my response to what the monster said to a London newspaper, "What a pathetic way to get attention! I've already given far more than he ever will to charity, and this whole event is nothing but a fraud."

I could only think of one reply to that hateful remark. "Well, since Mr. Pearce is such a philanthropist who has done so much for so many, I am happy to invite him to Paris. Layla can draw his eye, and maybe she can see the truth of his intentions from within," I said sarcastically.

To that offer, the Englishman never responded, but the public bickering cemented our rivalry, and the general population began to see him as the villain he was.

Since Layla's choice of medium was charcoal, we settled on a black and white theme for the table arrangements, the bar, the studio, and the staff attire. Only Layla was excused from it, as she wanted to wear the garb of her people, a red cotton Shuka that wrapped around her torso. She also wore a dozen colorful beaded necklaces and several bracelets on her lower arms, as well as some elongated leather earrings. Her most important accessory, though, was her winning smile, which I knew would give her artwork a run for its money.

The gallery was packed from the minute the doors opened till the minute we had to drag people out. Ultimately, the exhibition brought in an astounding $150,000, enough to construct and open three schools in Layla's village and the surrounding areas. Over the next four months, Ana frequently visited Kenya, and the schools finally opened, with Layla set up to be in charge of their operation. No longer would the children of that village be forced to sit on dusty cloths on the ground; now, they would sit at desks of their own, learning the lessons that would carry them to happier, more productive lives than their parents had ever known.

When Ana returned from Kenya, she had a lot to say. "Sebastian, the children were so happy," she said. "You should have seen them! We can't stop there though. There is so much more we can do."

"Like what?" I asked, eager to hear her ideas, because she was always so brilliant and insightful.

She looked at me with a wicked smile in her eyes, one I was sure Layla would have expertly captured on paper. "Well, first of all, I think we should have a child of our own, someone to continue our work after us."

A year later, we were blessed with a healthy baby girl, our angel Juliette.

Chapter Eight

Captain Marcel received his $1,500,000 on January 4, 1994, just as I promised. Half of that amount came from the sale of the naked boy statue by Constantin Brâncuși. I withdrew the remaining $750,000 out of my bank account, from my savings after many years of hard work. The captain had sold his flat a few years back, and he was off living his life happily in Crete, so I wired the money to him and was happy to be relieved of the debt I'd been carrying for all those years.

Two years later, I cemented the ownership and future of my gallery by buying the space from its owners. They were happy to be free of it, since they were so far away in Canada, and it was all 100 percent mine from that point forward.

The gallery continued to excel, and the exhibitions we'd scheduled at the beginning of the year were successful. Of course we had our ups and downs, the happy and sad moments, the hills and valleys common to all human life, but for the most part, it was a pleasant routine we were all comfortable with. One rainy night, though, that symphony of life was interrupted by the blaring sirens of firetrucks coming down our street and the subsequent sobs of our little Juliette, who showed up at our bedroom door, frightened of the noise.

I hurried out to the living room and threw open one of the windows. As soon as I did, our place was filled with the stench of smoke and the sound of another fire engine, its loud sirens echoing so loud through the streets that it literally rattled the closed windows of our flat. I put my head out to see where the trucks were headed, only to be horrified by the sight of billows of thick smoke rolling out of my gallery. "Ana!" I screamed, then quickly shoved my arms into my robe and ran down the stairs.

The firefighters were already at my business, trying to break down the door with their big hammers, banging as hard as they could. Black smoke and flames filled the inside. "No!" I screamed, trying to push my way in, but the firefighters forbade that and pulled me back. Hopelessly, I stared at the inferno in disbelief, along with the gathering crowd of neighbors and onlookers.

Three strong firefighters pulled a big hose from one of the trucks and used it to send a high-powered blast of water into the flames. In answer to their efforts, the fire released more smoke, and even taller, stronger, hotter flames licked up and out. A few other firefighters pulled a hose from the second firetruck. Finally, the flames began to settle, and the smoke became lighter and wispier. They continued soaking the place till there was only ash and smoking embers as evidence of the tragedy.

In all that chaos and noise, with all the screaming of the crowd, the splashing of the hoses, the shouting of the firefighters, and the crackling of the flames, I saw my whole life vanishing before me. Ana and Juliette stood silently beside me, each squeezing one of my hands, watching as the brave men did the best they could to save my gallery. I felt as helpless as I did that day so long ago, when I first walked into Ana's hospital room in Miami.

"We will get through this," my dear wife said in a choked whisper, but I could not muster a response for her.

An hour later, the fire was completely out, and the firemen left in their trucks. It took a while for the police to investigate the scene, but they deemed the cause to be related to the electrical circuitry. "It seems some rain leaked inside and caused a short. The circuit exploded, and...well, this," said one of the investigators. Then, after I signed a few statements and disclaimers, they allowed me to enter the gallery to assess the damage.

The reception area was completely destroyed. My leather sofas were nearly melted to the floor, the walls were charred and black, the floors were flooded, and debris and shattered glass were strewn everywhere. I broke out in a thick sweat, partly from the residual heat and partly from the emotional turbulence I felt.

I was almost unable to go on, and my feet felt like they weighed a ton as I made my way to the next two rooms. I was heartbroken to see that all the Gomez paintings had been burned to ash, with the exception of one; that lone treasure was still hanging, but it was damaged beyond repair. I knew that not even Professor Schmidt and I could salvage it, not even if we worked on it for 100 years.

Every second felt like a year as I forced myself to take each step. I didn't want to inure myself, and my shoes were soaked with water already. Both glass doors of the main gallery had shattered in the heat, and the red carpet was saturated with filthy, dirty water and soot. The walls were a bit smoke damaged, but the room was not totally victimized by the fire. That was one blessing in the midst of my heartbreak. I felt a small ping of optimism, and for just a moment, felt my soul come back to my body.

I ran to the office area, which was not as hot as the other rooms. I put my hand on the door of the safe room, and it felt normal. I unlocked it and turned the big wheel that allowed me to walk inside. I knew the fire could not get inside that safe, but I was worried that the heat might have damaged the paint. To my pleasant surprise, all twenty-four precious pieces were miraculously intact. Finding a half-smile again, I walked out and locked the safe. I closed the office door and went back to the gallery, where I found Professor

Schmidt sitting on a small chair, looking around at the mess.

"The paintings?" he questioned as soon as he caught sight of me.

"They're okay," I replied.

"Good. That safe was a good investment, Sebastian. I called the insurance company as soon as Ana told me about the fire. They will stop by around noon. Don't move anything. You know how those insurance agents are, always trying to make any excuse to get out of paying claims."

"The official police report says it happened because of that switch up front. They're probably right. Look at that hole on the left," I said as I moved close to where the circuit once was.

"That boy will be devastated," the professor said, pointing to the partially recognizable painting, the only survivor in that collection.

"Yes, I know. I notified him, and he should be here in an hour," I said.

It was a sad situation for us, but it was even worse for Gomez, because it was the opening day of his week-long exhibition. He was a short kid from Lisbon, only 20 years old. His cousin, Ricardo, practically had to drag him to Paris to meet us. Ricardo was the proof that artistic flair ran in the family, for we'd held an exhibition for him the previous year. His large landscape paintings were a big success, and we had high hopes for Gomez as well.

The day Gomez arrived, he was wearing dark blue jeans and plain white shirt, every wrinkle ironed out. His blond hair had a buzz cut, as if he'd served in the military, and he wore thick, brown glasses. He only spoke a few words and didn't make eye contact with Professor Schmidt or me. I had met hundreds of artists, but none of them produced work like his. He was a study in contradiction; it was difficult to believe that such a dull, plain young man could produce such explosive colors, and opalescent reflections. Whatever life he lacked in his own existence, he portrayed it vividly in his drawings. "He had a bit of a troubled childhood and was always bullied at school," Ricardo told us privately one day. "I guess this is his way of answering to that."

The exhibition at our gallery was supposed to put fourteen of his works on display for all the world to see. Finally, his work of three years would see the light. What we didn't know was that the light it would see would be orange and yellow and red, because that fire had other plans for the fate of shy Gomez's work.

The kid was stunned when he entered the gallery and saw only one ruined painting remaining.

"I am so very sorry, Gomez," I said as tears streamed down his cheeks. "The fire left...well, nothing."

He did not say a word and only sniffled and continued crying.

"I promise that once you have some new work to present, we will hold a huge exhibition for you. Here," I said, holding a check out to him. "It's $30,000, to pay you for your hard work."

The boy still did not speak, nor did he move.

"Take it, son. You deserve it. You are extremely talented for a young man your age. A long, successful path lies ahead of you in the art world, and we will be here when you are ready to try again," Professor Schmidt said as he took the check out of my hand and placed it in Gomez's palm.

"Mother will be happy about the money," he finally said, but he didn't sound very happy himself. "But as for me, no one will ever know. No one will ever even care." He then took one last look at the sad painting that remained, then walked out of what was left of my gallery.

Promptly at noon, the insurance agents arrived and inspected the premises. They asked me a few questions, then took a copy of the police report with them when they left.

"It seems we will need to close for some time," I said to my cohort.

"Well, that means more rest and a few more boring chess matches for me," he said, then walked away, using his cane to shove the wet, burnt remnants out of his way.

I offered to drive him home, but as usual, he refused. Despite the fact that he was 82, he was rather healthy, like a man 20 years younger.

Ana brought me a cheese sandwich and a mug of coffee. She asked about Gomez and what the insurance people said, then asked, "When are you coming home, Sebastian? You've had a long, tiring day. We all have."

"I will be there soon, my love. I just... I need to be alone for a while. Why don't you take Juliette to the park? She's only a child, and she's seen too much bad today, just like the rest of us."

After my wife and daughter left, I pushed the broken front table aside. Under one of the separated legs, I saw the photograph of our opening day, still in its frame. The glass was cracked in the middle, but the picture itself was fine. I carefully removed the shards, took the photograph out, and stared at it.

It had been eighteen years since that lovely day. We were all together then, but not all of those dear souls remained.

My mother was smiling in her wheelchair, maybe the happiest she'd ever been in that long, white dress of hers. She had left us five years ago, died peacefully in her sleep. My Juliette went in her grandmother's room to try to wake her, like she did every day, but none of us would ever speak to her again after that morning.

I looked at Akram Shukri and Mrs. Stanley, a great artist and an iron woman. Both of those good people had also passed.

My eyes then fell on my dear friend and savior, Ivan, who'd taken his last breath two and a half years ago. I had the privilege to see him a few months before that, and I noticed that he'd lost a lot of weight, so much that he looked like a skeleton. He was content about his fate when he was diagnosed with lung cancer, the disease that claimed him within a year. Idris and I were honored to be his pallbearers, to carry him in his coffin, to his final resting place.

Hakan was still among the living, but after he married a Colombian woman he met in Argentina, the couple moved to Bogota, and I hadn't heard from him since, not in over a decade.

At least I still have my Ana, Antoine, Émilie, Professor Schmidt, and the big man, I thought as I placed the cherished memory in my pocket. I then went back to work, lifting the broken pieces and debris from the dirty, soaked floor.

Several laborers were hired to help us get the place back in functioning order, and Patrice and I were busy working alongside them when Ricardo came in. He looked exhausted, and the long-sleeved black shirt didn't help. He was also holding an envelope in his hand.

"I am sad to announce that my cousin committed suicide last week," he said as his eyes filled with tears. "He left a note for you, and I wanted to bring it to you in person."

I collapsed to the floor and took the envelope, but my hands were shaking so terribly that I almost couldn't open it. When I did, I read it aloud: "Thank you, Monsieur Sebastian for believing in me, but life is cruel. Gomez."

I left the gallery and wandered in the streets, with no idea where I was heading. I just walked and walked, like a lost lunatic, until I circled back to the gallery three hours later. "Let the workers finish the week, then close this gallery and refund the fees to all our members. We will not bother to open again," I said sternly to Patrice.

For weeks after that, my only solace were the bottles of wine I consumed every day and night. No matter how hard Ana, Professor Schmidt, Antoine, and Émilie tried to cheer me up, none of it helped. "Tragedy is a natural part of life. Fires happen, Sebastian," they said, over and over again. "You are not to blame."

Their words were kind, but they had no effect on me. I could only think of Gomez and the motivation for him to take his life. *It was my fault because it was my electrical circuit, and there was nothing natural about that*, I thought. *I failed a young artist, and now he is dead.*

I barely ate anything, did not shave for weeks, and had an annoying attitude with everyone. When I realized my negativity was hurting sweet Juliette, I packed a bag and booked a flight to Reykjavik. Upon arrival, I rented a car, then drove to Vik, a small town in southern Iceland, with a population of about 500. I stayed in an isolated wood cabin on a hill that overlooked the tiny city.

I missed my friends and family, but I had to escape Paris. After the loss of my gallery and the news about Gomez, I could not stand the city, the paintings, or even the company of my loved ones. I felt like the walls were closing on me, and when I closed my eyes, all I could see was that young man in his thick, brown glasses, his perfectly ironed white shirt, and his dark blue jeans. I was sure I was losing my mind, going mad, and I thought nature might be the cure for what ailed me.

My ten days in Vik did calm me down to some extent. There, I slept a lot better, and, little by little, I stopped having nightmares and horrible daydreams about that boy who took his life.

Every morning, I awoke at six thirty, then brewed coffee and filled my stainless steel thermos. I packed a cheese sandwich and an apple, along with a one-liter water flask, and took off on my early hike into the Reynisfjall Mountains. It was a two-hour journey on foot, and from that spot, I had a 360-degree view of the natural beauty all around me. I admired the sea, the black, sandy beaches, the cliffs, and the basalt columns.

What fascinated me most, though, was peering through my binoculars and spying on the Atlantic puffins, the lundi, as the locals called them. I loved to watch the creatures dive into the sea, then fly away to their nests with their fresh catch in their colorful beaks. Iceland was home to more than half the world population of marvelous black and white birds. Their unique beaks, together with their flexible tongues, allowed the puffins to store dozens of fish at a time, so they could dive in and hunt again and again.

Something about watching the animals every morning eased my mind. When I closed my mind and imagined them flying through the sky, it brought healing to what was left of my soul.

After that, I continued my hike, moving downward, toward the shoreline. I carefully observed the geological changes that had happened to the rocks and caves over millions of years. The salty wind blowing off the ocean was a healing balm to my skin as I watched the waves lapping against the sand.

Sometimes, I thought of the gallery. I had started my project for three reasons: I had a passion for art, a desire to provide a portal for aspiring artists, and a need to give my mother something pleasant and productive to do after her sickness. Now, I'd lost my passion, one artist I'd tried to help was dead, and my mother was no longer with us either. My dream had morphed into a nightmare.

After an hour of toiling with those conflicting thoughts, around noon, I made my way back to the cabin. I cooked hot soup and grilled some fish I caught in the lake on my way back, mixed with the few vegetables I purchased from the market. Then, with my belly as full as my head, I fell asleep for a few hours.

In the evening, while the sun was still high in the sky, I returned to the village to visit the only bar. I drank a couple pints of local beer, then called Ana and Juliette, to let them know everything was all right. Then, I made my way back to my lonely home, passing the Vik church on the way. Every night, by the light of the fireplace in the cabin, I read one of the many Victor Hugo novels I had brought with me.

The locals gave me a nickname, the French Viking. I really couldn't blame them, because I knew I was quite a disheveled sight. My beard had grown up to where my sternum was, and my hair had reached lengths it hadn't seen since my boyhood. I remained there for over forty days, and I would have lingered for months, if not for a special visitor.

I was just returning from my daily hike when I saw her sitting on my porch. She was dressed fittingly in long, brown boots, white trousers, and a woven wool, maroon-colored top. The sunlight glistened in her short, red hair.

My heart beat almost audibly in my chest. My soul screamed for me to run to her, but my body refused to obey. All I could do was smile.

She smiled back, albeit softly, fully aware that I was still in deep pain. "Who is this grizzly bear approaching me?" she teased.

"How did you find the place?" I asked.

"There is only one crazy French guy in Vik, and everyone knows him here," she answered with a grin on her pretty face.

I moved close enough to hug her, so close I could smell her jasmine and neroli perfume. It had always been my favorite scent. "Juliette?" I said.

"Left her with Émilie. She is doing well, still asking about you. My driver is still in the city, so I have to drive back to Reykjavik to catch my flight back to Paris tomorrow afternoon. I just came to give you this," she said, then handed me dozens of letters, tied together with a ribbon. She also handed me an art magazine.

"What are these?" I asked, confused.

"Some are from gallery members, some from our artists. By the way, more than half refused to take their membership fees back. We still get calls every day about the gallery. Hakan himself called three times. Also, you should thumb through the magazine later. There is something interesting in it."

"Come inside, Ana," I invited as I tucked the bundle under my arm. "I've finally learned to make good coffee."

For a half-hour, we just looked into one another's eyes. There was so much to be said, but since we first met, then met again, our eyes had always done the talking. Although Ana was a different woman after the accident, our shared gazes still spoke volumes, and we both listened to what we were saying to each other, without a word between us. "You have such a special connection," my mother once said, and she was right.

"Thanks for coming, Ana. I know I have pushed you away, but I you know I—" I finally sputtered.

"I know, Sebastian," she chimed in before I could finish. "Me too. Don't you remember that you came for me, when I was in Miami."

"I know," I said quietly.

"Great coffee, by the way. I would buy that," she said. then she kissed me goodbye and walked out the door to head back to town.

I stared at my lovely wife as she became smaller and smaller, then faded in the distance. Once she was gone from sight, I went back inside, took out a knife, and cut the ribbon she'd tied around the letters and magazine.

Most of them were from members who hoped to visit the gallery soon, encouraging us to reopen. There were thank-you cards from artists, reminding me of the great help we were in securing their future. I read the dozens of messages one after another, then read them all again, with tears welling in my eyes.

Finally, I picked up the magazine. It was a few weeks old, but it looked intriguing, so I took a chair out to the porch and sat down to read it.

The main article was about the Fauvism era in its three peak years, between 1905 and 1908. The writer commented on the effect of André Derain and Henri Matisse on the movement. Another article discussed the Andy Warhol Museum in Pittsburgh, and it contained photos of some of the late American artist's work. That artist had some relatively odd views on the gay movement in the States, even though he lived an openly gay lifestyle himself.

When I flipped through the pages, I saw more news on paintings, auctions, and new gallery openings. The last article was the one that really caught my attention, the one I knew Ana had come all that way to bring for me.

Occupying half the page was a photograph of a familiar man in a dark gray suit and a red tie, sitting on a black leather chair. He was holding a black pipe in his hand, and there was a gallery of paintings behind him.

In the interview, Matthew Pearce bragged about all the artwork his gallery owned, as well as the museums he had done business with in the past. He went on and on about how Pearce Gallery gained possession of those treasures, and he boasted about how well they took care of the one-of-a-kind valuables.

The whole article boiled my blood, but one of his answers angered me so much that I literally threw the magazine down as soon as I read it. "Art should be protected the way one would protect their child," he said. "I worry about the important, irreplaceable, historical works under the ownership of Allure Gallerie. They recently had a fire, so it has become obvious that they do not offer the protection their treasures deserve. Personally, I think Mr. Sebastian should allow others to own and preserve those beauties. Pearce Gallery is ready to make him a very generous offer. We can only hope he will swallow his pride and contact us, for the sake of the art. To be honest, I have my doubts about the man. I am very suspicious of his relationship with the late Ivan Olic. They were close friends for years. A few months back, I was told from a source I trust about his alleged relationship with the mafia, during the Yugoslav wars. I quickly sold all the paintings I bought from him then, as I wanted nothing to do with art purchased with blood money."

I could not believe a professional magazine would publish such rubbish, and it infuriated me. Not only did he smudge my reputation, but he attacked Ivan, who was as clean as a man could be. When I read his spiteful assault, that dying passion within me reawakened. Just like that, as I knew Ana hoped I would, I threw on the first decent clothes I could find, ran to the local bar, made a few calls, and booked my flight back to Paris for the very next day.

Later that night, as I packed my bag, I was still steaming. "Now he's gone too far. I cannot let him get away with this anymore," I fumed. I was willing to fight him, to my last breath, for soiling the good reputation of me, of my gallery, and of a friend I desperately missed.

The next morning, I awoke before six, shaved my monstrous beard, then dropped the keys, and a little note of gratitude in the postal box of the owner, who lived in town next to the library. I took a bus to Reykjavik. From there, I grabbed a ten-minute taxi ride to the airport.

"Hey, I was wondering where you were," Ana said as she stood near the departure gate. "What took you so long?"

"The beard, my Red Queen. Blame it on the beard!" I said, and we kissed as we never had before, paying no regard to the audience of travelers around us.

When we got back home, Juliette made it clear that my hair was awful, so the first thing I did the next morning was fix that with a nice trim of my mop top. The second thing was to go pick up Professor Schmidt.

"How dare you?" he said, then tapped me twice on the leg with his cane, making it obvious how much he'd missed me.

We went straight to the gallery, and Patrice was already there, with a huge smile on his face. He'd been there since eight a.m., and he was clearly delighted to be back.

"Patrice, send word to everyone that the gallery will be open in two months. From that day on, the public will be invited to view the main collection for free, with no requirement for membership. We will install a library and café in the front, and we'll tear down the dividing wall and add a small kitchen. Someone please call the contractor and let him know I'd like to meet with him tomorrow."

"But what about—" Patrice tried, struggling to remember all of my urgent instructions.

"Also, I want you to get in touch with Sameer. Do you remember him? He's that Frenchman of Moroccan descendant. He exhibited with us back in 1988, and he is now very well known for his frescos. Tell him I'd like him to paint the ceiling and walls of our new library and find out how much he would charge. He knows I'll kill him if he overcharges!"

Patrice chuckled. "Anything else, Boss?"

"Yes. I want the library to be extravagant, full of books about art, so many people can benefit from it. We must include volumes about the artists we display in the main gallery, as well as everything related to avant-garde. We need lots of material on Cubism, abstract impressionism, landscape art... I want at least 500 books in there."

"That's a lofty goal," the professor said, "but a doable one. The world is full of books, maybe more books about art than the art itself! I have a few books I would be happy to donate to the cause."

"Good. Thank you, Professor," I said. "As for the café, it should be furnished with ten small, round, wooden tables that seat four. We need to hire a great, friendly barista, and we should have fresh pastry daily. You can leave the coffee selection to me," I said to Patrice as he struggled to catch up with all I'd said.

On one of Ana's trips to Kenya, she bought some coffee beans, and everyone loved and praised the beverage they produced. For that reason, I made sure to ask Ana to contact Layla, so she could arrange to send us a large quantity of that wonderful Kenyan coffee.

With the right amount of rainfall and year-round sunlight, the acidic soil in the highlands there provided perfect conditions for the growing of coffee plants. AA Kenyan coffee beans were considered mild. The coffee was intense, though, full-bodied, with pleasant aroma and notes of cocoa that made it special. I needed that to be offered in my café.

I also called my good friend Hakan and thanked him for his concern. "Do you have any contacts in the coffee industry, now that you've been such a jetsetter?" I asked him, with a smile in my voice that I hoped he could hear through the phone. "I'm looking for pure Colombian, as well as Central American geisha beans."

"I will have an answer for you within a few days, my friend," he promised.

After everyone left for the day, it was time for one of the most important calls in my life.

"Welcome back, Sebastian," Idris answered right away.

"Thanks, big man. I read Matthew Pearce's interview yesterday, and that jolted me back to reality. I can't believe his audacity."

"I know. If I was near him now, I would snap his back in half. I can't believe he said those things about Ivan. He did not know him well, but he knows all the good Ivan did for so many. His words were disgusting!"

"I know, my friend. Pearce is a monster."

"You know, Sebastian, the elderly facility restoration has really taken a chunk out of our finances lately. It looks as new and shiny as it did the day we opened it, but it has been expensive to correct the damage caused by the bombing. Before Ivan's death, I promised him I would finish it. It is done, but the maintenance is not cheap.

"I thought I had things under control, and work finally picked up back here after the war, but that weasel's interview affected our group more than you can imagine. A local paper here published the part about Ivan, you know that in Serbia, they are looking for any leads to war crimes. Our construction company was awarded the forty-five-kilometer restoration project on the highway stretching from Trogir to Omis, and a small bridge near that as well. It was good business, worth around $10,000,000, but the committee in charge, on suspicion of Ivan, took the project away from us and gave it to someone else, some group based in Zagreb," he said furiously.

"That's good, Idris," I replied.

"Good? Sebastian, have you heard anything I've said?" he replied, sounding a bit angry.

"Years ago, Idris, you told me about the circle of life, and I've never forgotten that conversation. It is time, my friend. It is time," I consoled.

"Time for what? Enlighten me, would you?" the giant said, his tone softening a bit.

"I think Matthew Pearce mistakenly thinks no one will stand up for Ivan, now that he's gone. Ivan's children sold the shipping business and moved to the States when the war escalated in 1993, and that made world news. Pearce obviously doesn't know about the construction group, nor is he aware that you are the sole owner, because Ivan left it to you."

"Where are you going with this, Sebastian?"

"Can you prove that all Ivan's businesses in the past were 100 percent clean, with no black spots anywhere?" I asked hopefully.

"Ivan was cleaner than everyone here. I have all the records to prove it, because he was also very organized. I still don't understand though," he said, sounding more interested in my proposition.

"If that is true, Idris, then I'm sure you also have all the details about the latest project, the contract that was taken from you. Can you support your accusations with numbers? Do you have documentation to attest to it?"

"Yes, and I think I understand now. You want me to sue him for damages, because of his interview," Idris concluded.

"Yes, but you will also sue the magazine. You will not be alone though. I will sue them separately as well, for defaming me and my business."

"Ah! I like that," my friend boomed, "but it will cost us. As I just told you, I don't have a lot of cash on hand to hire legal counsel or— "

"Don't worry about that. The magazine doesn't want to be dragged into a legal war, and they surely don't want the bad publicity. They have been publishing art for decades now, and they are well known in the industry. They may even try to blame the journalist, but in the end, they will pay any amount to settle out of court, to put the matter to rest. Then, we can use that money to continue our case against Matthew." I replied.

"The damn circle of life!" Idris said, with a big chuckle.

"Yes, the $12,000,000 damn circle of life," I parroted, laughing even louder.

Chapter Nine

The magazine settled within three months, as I predicted they would. I was compensated with a whopping $100,000 for my trouble, and Idris was granted ten times that. Three years later, though, we were still dealing with Matthew Pearce.

Pearce went with a big firm, and they did their best to drag the case along as slowly as possible. They used every trick in the book. Their lawyers came up with witnesses, documentation, and precedents from decades ago, trying to find any way to justify their client's screw-up. Fortunately, we were in a good position. We had the finances to see the process through, and we even rejected several attempts by his legal team to settle. One night, Matthew even called me himself and offered us a few million if we would drop the case. It was the first time the Englishman had spoken to me directly about the legal proceedings, and that revealed just how desperate he was. When I refused his deal, he became furious. "You are just a bunch of scavengers," he said when I told him I preferred to let the court handle it.

Meanwhile, Matthew's own reputation was rapidly swirling down the drain. Auction houses and other galleries began distancing themselves from him. On the contrary, our gallery saw even more success. Visitors enjoyed the café, where they sipped the best coffee available in Paris, and they loved spending time to learn from the hundreds of books in our library. They enjoyed all of that with an all-access gallery of masterpieces just a few feet away.

One day, I was enjoying a mug of my favorite Jamaican brew in the café, looking at a biography about Van Gogh. I was engulfed in a chapter about how many of the estimated 2,000 pieces by the man were still missing.

"Following the footsteps of a great man, are you?" Patrice asked.

"Footsteps?" I repeated, looking up at him curiously. After a moment of thought and another sip of strong coffee, then one more glance of the paintings in the book, I smiled and said, "Footsteps, footsteps, footsteps!"

"Uh, did I say something wrong?" Patrice asked, confused.

"No. In fact, that may have been the best thing you've said all year, maybe within a few years," I retorted. I got up and ran over to the barista for a refill, then hurried back to Patrice. "Do you know how many pieces I've acquired from auctions or private galleries since you joined?" I asked my faithful friend.

"Twelve," he was quick to answer.

"Right. Only a dozen in twenty years. Why?"

"I-I'm not sure," he stuttered, still confused.

"Patrice, I think the main reason is because we've always sought to buy art in the same places as everyone else, at the same time. Plus, we didn't have the money to compete. Does that sound right to you?"

Patrice nodded.

"We approached auctions and private galleries who offered their items to the whole market. The two times I took a different approach, I was very lucky. Remember what I gained from the captain and Mrs. Stanley? I can't take credit for the latter, as that was on Ivan's suggestion."

"What is your point, Sebastian?"

"My friend, I believe there are dozens or hundreds of pieces being stored somewhere, maybe owned by people who have no idea of their worth. Some may simply not know what to do with their valuable possessions. We should search for those people, seek out those people."

"How? How will we find them?" he asked.

"You already answered that question."

"I did?" he asked, confused again.

"Footsteps, Patrice! We will follow the footsteps of the greats, and I am sure we will find art that has never been seen before."

"Hmm. You may be on to something, but it is a big ocean to fish in, Sebastian. It could take months, years, maybe decades," Patrice replied before he fetched his own cup of coffee and sat down to join me.

"As Mrs. Stanley would have said, nonsense! You are an encyclopedia of art history yourself, and so is Professor Schmidt. We can focus on only a few artists, dig up everything we can on them, every little detail of their lives. We'll explore their trips, their relationships, and see where that leads. You have all the time in the world, and I will give you all the finances you need, including any assistants you need," I said just before I took the final gulp of my second cup.

Three months later, Patrice was leading his team of three on the project, including himself, Professor Schmidt, and Daniella, an Italian historian who majored in the impressionist movement, a smart, single lady from Milan. Patrice knew her because they'd both attended some of the same lectures many years prior.

The second new addition was Michael, a graduate of Oxford who'd been living in Paris for nearly a year, earning his master's. He'd studied avant-garde and its effects on art. Now, we saw him in the café daily, learning all he could from many books while sipping his favorite chamomile tea. The young Englishman was a perfect fit.

We offered Daniella and Michael a hefty contract, and a 10 percent cut of any artwork they helped us locate. We also assured them that they would have all the financial support they needed for their worthy pursuit. "Trips, books, research... Whatever you need, we'll be sure you get it," I told them.

At times, all three would study together till the wee hours, with dozens of books spread out between them. Other times, I didn't see any of them for weeks, because they were busy roaming around various cities, researching, visiting other museums, libraries, and universities.

Professor Schmidt and I met with them once a month so they could fill us in on their progress. We usually met at a small restaurant nearby, so we could discuss things over a bottle of wine.

After six months, they began to compare notes and connect the dots on anything any of them had missed. Once they had that information, they started to determine what steps to follow for the next six months.

At our first annual meeting, I set the café up as something resembling a classroom, with a large whiteboard and lots of colorful markers at the front.

Professor Schmidt, Ana, Antoine, Émilie, and I listened as the team presented all they had learned, giving us a deep look into the lives of the three greats they'd chosen, Picasso, Modigliani, and Renoir. They also gave us an overview of their plans going forward.

Daniella was the first to speak, and she seemed very comfortable in front of all of us, sitting next to the whiteboard. "I was assigned Renoir," she began, "so I first visited his birthplace in Limoges, Haute-Vienne, in west central France. I learned that the artist's father was a tailor in that area, till the family moved to Paris."

She went on to tell us that her next visit was Renoir's old home around rue d'Argenteuil, in central Paris, the place where he grew up, quite near The Louvre. She met with descendants of Renoir's neighbors and childhood friends, to see what stories had been passed down. Impressively, Daniella also dug up some information on the porcelain factory Renoir worked in until 1858.

Next, she followed his footsteps to Ecole des Beaux Arts, where he studied. She discovered the impact they had on him. She talked to us about Renoir's beginnings as an artist and his time under Charles Gleyre, who taught him and the likes of Claude Monet, Alfred Sisley, and Frédéric Bazille.

Next, Daniella mentioned Renoir's first love, Lise Tréhot, his preferred model between 1866 and 1872.

After her relationship with Renoir ended, Lise married Georges Brière de l'Isle. The couple had four children together, and those children inherited Renoir's works from their mother. Daniella underlined the whole family on the board and wrote, "Two works, maybe more? Need more investigation."

From there, she went on to talk about Renoir's experience during the Franco-Prussian War and his time at the Fontainebleau area with the family of Jules Le Cœur. She also explained her visit to Algeria, a place Renoir frequented. She shared her findings from her trip to Palermo, where Renoir met and drew the composer Richard Wagner. She spoke about Suzanne Valadon, another of Renoir's models. "She was an artist herself, the first female painter to be admitted to the Société Nationale des Beaux-Arts," Daniella said. She then spoke of Aline Charigot, his first wife, and the couple's three sons, Pierre, Jean, and Claude, as well as Aline's cousin and nurse, Gabrielle Renard, who lived with them for a long while.

After she concluded her annual report, Daniella spoke about her next steps. Her initial instinct was to follow the footsteps of Lise Tréhot and her family, then Aline Charigot her three sons and cousin, Gabrielle Renard.

We all had questions that she was happy to answer. Patrice and Michael shared her opinion, but Patrice added, "The family of Jules Le Cœur should not be ignored, as Renoir was close to them for nearly a decade."

Picasso was Michael's territory, mostly because he was fluent in Spanish and because the painter had been part of his ongoing studies for the past few years.

Michael took his place near the whiteboard and explained that he also started with the artist's birthplace, Malaga. "I went to Picasso's first home, spoke to those in charge of it now, and I talked to many people in the neighborhood to gain a better understanding of the art master as a child." He learned quite a bit about Picasso's father, Don José Ruiz y Blasco. "He was a painter himself, as well as a professor of art at the School of Crafts. He also worked at the local museum, and he was Picasso's biggest supporter and teacher in the early years," Michael said.

Next, he told of his findings in Barcelona, where Picasso lived alone for some time in a small room, to focus more on his art. Picasso considered Barcelona his home, as it was where he felt the most comfortable. "There is much to be understood about his time there," Michael said, "and he forged many significant relationships in that city. I will definitely return there in the future, to learn more about it."

Michael then traveled to Madrid, where he visited Real Academia de Bellas Artes de San Fernando, one of the most renowned art academies in Spain. He met the museum director, went through the archives, and noted all he could about Picasso and his works.

"After 1900, Picasso lived here, in Paris," he said. "His roommate, Max Jacob, was a journalist and poet and helped young Picasso settle in. This was his home from then on, though he did visit Barcelona a lot for a few years. The suicide of his good friend Carlos Casagemas inspired Picasso's gloomy, somber paintings, rendered in shades of blue and aquamarine, best known as his Blue Period."

Michael spoke to us about the man's Rose Period as well. Fernande Olivier, a bohemian artist who became his mistress, was the feature of one of his many paintings. Next, we discussed Picasso's relationship with the Stein family, American art collectors. Michael Stein, his wife Sarah, Leo Stein, Gertrude Stein, and her nephew Allan Stein all added Picasso's works to their collections. Gertrude later became the principal patron, acquiring all his artwork.

Michael then talked about Picasso's relationship within the Montmartre and Montparnasse quarters, with the likes of André Breton, poet Guillaume Apollinaire, and writer Alfred Jarry. He touched on Picasso's new love, Eva Gouel, who died only a few years after the two of them met. She had a profound effect on his work as well. His first wife, Olga Khokhlova, gave birth to a son, Paulo. Marie-Thérèse

Walter was the mother of his daughter Maya, and Françoise Gilot gave birth to Picasso's two other children, Claude, and Paloma, who were still alive and well.

Michael's impressive homework came to an end at that point, and Patrice took over.

Patrice loved Modigliani. Although the painter lived only to the age of 35, his short life was rich with experiences. Patrice did not take as long as the other two before, but he did present his story to us in a different way. On the board, he wrote several facts, in the form of simple points:

Livorno, Guglielmo Micheli.

Accademia di Belle Arti di Venezia, Venice.
Introduced to hashish. Started bohemian wild life.

Oscar Ghiglia. Seven years senior to Modigliani.
Mentor during teenage years.

Paris from 1906.

Lived in the poverty commune, Le Bateau-Lavoir, in Montmartre.

Started a studio with Jacob Epstein, American of Jewish-Polish descent. Moved to London later and became British. Not much there on the two, but they shared a studio.

Frequent affairs, heavy drinking, daily absinthe and hashish use.

Drew hundreds of pieces that were damaged by artist or lost due to constant movement.

Anna Akhmatova, Russian poet, married to Nikolay Gumilyov. First serious love for Modigliani. One-year affair. Needs further study.

Paul Guillaume, art dealer and friend.

Jules Pascin and Moïse Kisling both lived in his building. Moïse and wife modeled for him. Immigrated to the States. Visit.

Nina Hamnett, affair. Wild, like Modigliani. Two were seen drunk together and often smoked hashish. Later Nina married Edgar de Bergen. Interesting couple to follow.

Léopold Zborowski, primary art dealer. Paris exhibition and Nice trip. Requires extensive study.

Jeanne Hébuterne, lover and wife till death. Main focus.

After writing all that, Patrice talked for only five minutes about what he had written. He then went back to his seat and opened the floor for questions, which he readily answered.

"This is a great surface we have just started to scratch, a long road we have just begun to travel. Nevertheless, I am very pleased with your progress," I said, raising a toast to conclude the evening.

Several years passed as Patrice, Daniella, and Michael delved deeper. Some names were discarded from their initial lists, when they determined those leads led nowhere. Daniella was the first to make a major find, three Renoir sketches in Algeria. She came upon them after staying in the city of Casbah for more than a month, following a hint she'd found.

Daniella turned that place upside down, till she encountered a small, old bakery around the Mosquée de la Pêcherie, the same bakery where Renoir bought his daily bread over a century ago. The baker she met inherited the business from his father, who had also inherited it from his. He showed her many letters and some paperwork that belonged to his grandfather during the French occupation. It was in that paperwork that she found the sketches. It was certainly not the vast treasure we had been waiting for, but it was a good breakthrough, a prize for the gallery that would garner some cash for us and for Daniella.

We displayed the sketches for six months before they sold for around $250,000, to a private collector from New York. Despite the stable cash flow from the café and library book sales, that artwork was our first major sale since we rehomed Brâncuşi's statue six years earlier. It was a good start to the new millennium, and it encouraged us to continue following in those footsteps.

Several months later, I received more good news from Idris. "Pearce is willing to pay me $12,000,000 to close the case," he informed me. Then, a day later, I received a call from Pearce's lawyer, who made an offer I could not refuse, $450,000. Neither of us could believe our sudden good fortune. Matthew would have never offered those figures a few months prior, but three weeks later, we were fully compensated, just as my enemy promised.

After the case closed, we fished around for the reason behind the settlement. It turned out that Mr. Pearce was caught up in a fierce divorce battle with his wife, and he did not want us on his back as well. She was fighting him for $24,000,000, half of his $48,000,000 estimated net worth. I also discovered that he had to sell some of his paintings in order to fund our compensation. Now, they were owned by an old friend of his, Steven Yun, who operated a well-known gallery in China, one of the biggest galleries in Asia.

"The circle of life, Idris," I reminded my friend. "He learned his damn lesson, and how he has too much on his plate to bother us again. We can consider that chapter closed," I said as we celebrated with a bottle of champagne, in honor of our mutual friend and benefactor, dear Ivan.

Months later, it was all over the news that Pearce's wife had financially drained him, to the point where he had to declare bankruptcy. Matthew left London, and it was rumored that he settled somewhere in the Caribbean. He had to have some money stashed away for that, but he lived a low profile from that point on, and he didn't concern me anymore.

Ana and Juliette were in Kenya to open the eighth school since the effort began. This time, Ana wanted our daughter by her side, so she would understand the importance of the work they were doing for such an admirable humanitarian cause. Patrice, Michael, and Daniella were still traveling, hoping to find more hidden masterpieces.

All alone in the café, Professor Schmidt and I watched the latest news about the fall of Baghdad, declared by the Americans just two days ago, on the historic day of April 9, 2003. The video on the TV showed a city in chaos, with crazed crowds running and looting, taking whatever they felt was theirs from the old regime. When they broke into the Iraqi museums, ancient statues crashed to the ground and paintings were ripped out of their frames.

"No!" Professor Schmidt shouted, standing from his chair. "No, no, no! All that history, all that art. Nooo!" the old man screamed hysterically, pointing his cane at the TV.

I neared him and tried to calm him down, but he would not stop shouting. When I saw his cane fall from his hand, then the professor falling with it, I was shocked and terrified. His eyes were open, but he was completely motionless. I slapped him, trying desperately for any response, but he did not acknowledge me at all.

Not sure what else to do, I grabbed my cell phone and called for an ambulance. While I waited for them to arrive, I checked his pulse and was relieved to feel one, though it was very weak. I tried to administer the little first aid I knew, but he didn't react to it at all.

A few minutes later, the ambulance arrived, and the medics put him on a gurney and rushed him into the emergency vehicle. They allowed me to climb inside beside him.

A few minutes later, as the ambulance raced to the hospital, the medic beside Professor Schmidt looked at me. "I am sorry," he said.

For that, I had no words. My mentor, my father figure had passed away. The worst of it was that he didn't fall prey to illness or old age; in the end, it was his passion for art and its preservation that killed him.

A grand funeral was held for the man who'd served the art community in Paris for over fifty years. Over 500 people were there to honor him and pay their respects. Then, we buried the professor in his final resting place, Montparnasse Cemetery.

I wasn't really surprised to learn that he left everything to me in his Will. I was now the owner of his flat and all his belongings, as well as a note that his lawyer handed to me, a letter, dated three months prior. I instantly opened it and read:

Sebastian,

Thank you for the years. A year after I retired from The Louvre, I thought my life would have no meaning. Here we are decades later, hard at work.

Don't stop looking!

Schmidt

P.S. Lately, I have noticed you walking with a limp in your left knee. Please take my cane. It has helped me for years, and it will help you too.

After the funeral, the events that led to his death kept in playing my mind. It was awful that the last thing Professor Schmidt saw was a few angry looters, destroying the heritage of the world.

With that on my mind, I hurried to my gallery and took Akram Shukri's *The Eye* off the wall and placed it in the safe. "Patrice," I said, "find anyone from the Shukri family in Baghdad and tell them our gallery would like to gift Akram's painting to the museum there once things are back to normal."

A month later, Patrice managed to get in touch with one of Akram's nephews, and the message was passed on. Thousands upon thousands of people had admired the painting in Paris during its stay in our gallery. It was only fair that Iraqi art lovers could enjoy his work too. His nephew was thrilled with the idea, and just a month later, the painting was safely in the family's hands, with a promise to be delivered to the Iraqi museum upon its reopening.

Nothing was the same after Professor Schmidt left, and his absence was felt every day. I tried to bear his goals in mind, and that goal was well within reach one day when Michael called to tell me he'd finally found something.

"Daniella and I narrowed down a lead to Apollinaire. He gave Picasso the original manuscript of *The Exploits of a Young Don Juan* in 1907, when the two were close friends. We were certain that Picasso had to give him something in return. We got nowhere with Eva Gouel and the Stein family, so we teamed up to dig into this."

"Tell me more," I encouraged.

"Well, there were many associated with Apollinaire but from what we know about his lifestyle and his weakness for the fairer sex, we've gleaned that he had three women in his life. There was Marie Laurencin, his muse, Madeleine Pages, his fiancée, and Jacqueline Kolb, his wife.

"We got nowhere with the first two women, but yesterday, we located the son of a man who had Apollinaire's as a tenant, a drug addict named Didier. The man has been in and out of jail, guilty of many felonies like drug abuse, minor theft... The list goes on and on. We tracked him down through some patrons of a local bar. He lives in a small studio in Bordeaux. He thought Daniella and I were cops, but we told him we are just journalists writing about Apollinaire and that we're aware of his father's acquaintance with the late painter's wife. We gave him a little money, and I don't even want to imagine what he'll do with it, but it enticed him to talk. He told us about his father, their relationship, and many other things."

"Does he know the whereabouts of his father's belongings?" I chimed in.

"Well, he said his father died while he was still in jail. After his release, he took hold of his studio and many boxes of photographs, clothes, papers, and a painting or some artwork. When he mentioned the painting, Daniella and I showed him some photos of artwork by different greats like Pollock, Monet, Rembrandt, and Picasso. We asked if anything his father had looked similar to those, and you'll never guess what he did."

"What?"

"He chose Picasso's *Portrait of Daniel-Henry Kahnweiler*, the one Picasso created during the time he was acquainted with Apollinaire!"

"Very interesting, Michael. Amazing indeed!" I said enthusiastically. "Have you told Patrice about this?"

"Not yet. He's in Nice. Daniella and I are here, waiting for you," he said, then hung up the phone.

That night, I could not sleep. *Have we finally found the big prize, after seven long years?* I wondered. *Professor, we might have done it!*

I arrived the next day and joined Daniella and Michael so we could head straight over to talk to the guy.

Monsieur Didier was in his late forties. He looked and smelled drunk, and he was dressed sloppily in a ragged shirt and loose gray trousers. His beard was as messy as his apparel, and his teeth were yellow. His ramshackle appearance made him look much older than he probably was.

As soon as we walked into the bar near his place and all the introductions were made, he started blabbing about his father. "My father owned the flat Jacqueline Kolb lived in for over ten years," he said. He then mentioned the boxes his father had left behind. "I had no interest in digging through the old man's junk, but a few months ago, I was curious and dumped a few of them out. If memory serves me correctly, I think I saw a few rolled paintings, one of them similar to what you showed me."

"Okay," I said, not sure we could believe him.

"Look, I don't want trouble. I don't understand these things, and I don't care about anything my father ever had or did. Why would I? He never cared about me one bit," Didier said, then chugged a big swallow of beer.

I handed him several hundred Euros and assured him, "Nothing but good will come from this, sir. We just need to check what you have."

"Then you'd better come with me," he said. "It's close, just five minutes away on foot."

His studio was dark, and the forest-green curtains blocked any light from coming in. When he flicked on the lights, it became clear why he preferred the darkness: The place was filthy. There were cigarette butts and empty beer bottles everywhere. His meager furnishings included a small TV next to an untidy bed and a big, brown wardrobe. All in all, it was a very depressing space, and I couldn't fathom anyone wanting to live in it.

Without hesitation, because he was anxious for us to be on our way, Didier opened the wardrobe. He pulled out a box, then dug through it till he came across a folded painting, which he handed to me. "This is it," he said.

I took the painting and moved over to the window, then opened the curtains so I could see it better, with more natural light. I looked at it carefully, turning the painting over a few times. I then took out another 100 euros and handed them to Didier.

Daniella and Michael looked at each other, then looked back at me, with happiness, joy, and disbelief in their eyes.

"Thank you for your time," I said as I folded the painting and put it back in the box.

"Sebastian, why... What are you doing?" Michael asked furiously.

"It isn't authentic," I said. I then turned and walked down the stairs, with the aid of Professor Schmidt's cane.

Right on my heels, Michael raised his voice to me for the first time since I'd met him. "Didn't you see those brown colors, those angles, the mirror image of an old lady? It's in his cubism style."

"It is a fake. If you don't believe me, pay the man a few hundred more, take it, and go have it checked for yourself. It's yours if you want it," I said.

Michael was apparently one of those people who took failure very hard, because I never saw him again after that. After a few months, he conceded that Didier's painting was a fake, and he apologized to me in an email and thanked me for helping him to follow his dreams for so many years.

When Michael asked how I knew right away that the painting was only a replica, I simply answered, "I was trained by the best. Picasso was right-handed, but the strokes near the signature in that painting were made by someone left-handed."

Daniella also left us a month later, because she felt she no longer had the passion or desire to continue. "I can't help feeling as if you're heading into an endless, dark tunnel, with no light ahead," she said.

With the two of them no longer part of our team, Patrice and I spent two weeks discussing our next steps. We diligently combed through all the information they'd gathered over the years. After many give-and-take and back-and-forth sessions, we agreed that the easiest path was that of Modigliani. Patrice felt he was still largely undiscovered. Many historians stated that the artist damaged much of his own work or sold it to random buyers for a few francs. "I'm sure something is out there," Patrice said, "and it's only a matter of time before we stumble upon a discovery of great worth."

The weeks stretched into a month, and the months stretched into a year, then two. Still, none of the leads we had took us anywhere, but we kept trying, if only to honor the professor's wishes and all his hard work.

As Juliette grew, she became more interested in our work, and she spent hours with Patrice as he researched Modigliani. She was excellent at finding resources on the internet, and that was a benefit to Patrice, because he was old school. Juliette was enrolled to start college in three months, but the project kept her busy, and she seemed to enjoy it. "It's fun, like detective work," she said. Her energy was also an asset; she was as lively as her mother in all pursuits.

I didn't complain too much, but I was personally growing a bit disheartened, feeling quite like Daniella did. I wasn't sure if it had something to do with my age or with the many years spent on the hunt or if it had more to do with the fact that I felt I'd abandoned Ana in our quest to help the people of Africa. Eight schools in twenty years was disappointing. I had wasted hundreds of thousands of dollars on my art pursuit, and that began to weigh heavily on me. It also began to show in my attitude; I was quick-tempered and less patient before, and Juliette often asked, "Why are you so grumpy, Father?"

One night, Juliette missed dinner with her mother and me because she was working late with Patrice at the gallery again. The same thing happened the night before, and because of it, Juliette woke up late and forgot to bring some papers I needed. This time, I got upset, so right after dinner, I threw a coat on over my pajamas and stormed off to the gallery. The doors were locked, but since I saw lights on, I used my key and went inside.

Patrice and Juliette had pushed three of the café tables together and were busily working, my daughter on her laptop and Patrice examining loads of papers and boxes.

"Again, Juliette? Your mother made a special dinner for you, all your favorite food, and you didn't show up again. It is late, and it is time to go. You, too, Patrice. Your family must be saying the same," I said, looking at both of them.

"Give me an hour, Dad. I just printed dozens of Modigliani's photographs, and we're examining them one by one," she said.

"She's right, Sebastian. It won't take long," Patrice replied.

"As I said, it is late. You can finish tomorrow," I said, my voice growing stern and impatient.

"Just one hour, Dad," Juliette pleaded again.

"Now!" I said angrily, tapping my cane on one of the boxes.

When the box fell to the floor and some photographs spilled out, Juliette sighed and quickly closed her laptop, and Patrice was instantly on his feet.

I realized I had lost my temper, so I bent down to pick up the mess I'd made. One of the photos was of Modigliani and his wife Jeanne. Another was him standing next to Picasso. In the last, I could not tell who the others were. "Who is this?" I asked, showing the photograph to Patrice.

"That was taken outside an old restaurant in Nice. It's still there. Next to Modigliani are Zborowski, his art dealer, and his fellow artist, Foujita," Patrice replied timidly, as if he feared I might shout at him again.

"And the girl?" I asked, pointing.

"Don't know, just a child playing, I guess," he replied, calming a bit.

I looked at the photograph again. "Give me the magnifying glass," I said to Juliette.

"Sure, Dad."

Once she handed it to me, I used it to take a closer look at the photo. "Let me see some of the other pictures of him," I said.

"What is it, Sebastian?" Patrice asked.

After I looked at each photo at least a dozen times, I answered, "In most of them, Modigliani looked directly at the photographer. In this one, he tilted his head a bit to the right," I said, holding the photos together.

"So?" Patrice replied.

"Look at the girl through this magnifying glass. It appears she was trying to say something."

They took turns observing the photograph and agreed with what I said.

"Now, Patrice, stand a few feet in front of me, with your back toward me. The minute I say your name, turn your head to look at me. Juliette, grab that cute Nokia phone of yours and take a photo of Patrice the minute I call his name."

A few minutes later, we looked at the photos she had taken. Patrice's head was tilted halfway when I called his name, just as Modigliani's was in his photograph.

"Pack your bags," I said. "We are going to Nice Saturday, to find this mysterious woman and see what she has to say."

Chapter Ten

It had been nearly ten years since I had last visited Nice. The last time, Ana, Juliette, and I were there on a short vacation, to enjoy the beaches and the beautiful French Riviera. This time, our visit had little to do with leisure.

From the airport, we rented a car and went straight to the restaurant. Patrice had gone there in the past, as well as many other locations in the city, trying to gather any information he could about Modigliani. "They serve the best oysters in Nice," he affirmed.

The restaurateur, Monsieur Gerard, had been entertaining guests there for over forty years, after he took over for his father-in-law who had opened the place back in 1910. Gerard welcomed us kindly when we arrived.

I immediately explained the nature of our visit and showed him the old photo taken outside his place.

"Ah, yes, I have that hanging somewhere in the back," he said proudly. "Come with me."

We walked to his wall of fame and saw snapshots of the many celebrities, presidents, and artists who had graced the eatery with their presence over the years. Among the many painters who had dined there were Picasso and Matisse.

"This picture was taken when my father-in-law still owned the place, probably between 1915 and 1917," he said as he took the original off the wall.

"Do you know who the little girl is?"

The man looked at it closely. "I am sorry, but no. I wasn't even born then," he replied.

As we were talking, an older couple entered the restaurant and sat down at a table nearby. Monsieur Gerard was quick to greet them and to serve them a carafe of white wine from the bar.

I caught the old couple staring at us, and then the old man stood and walked over to join us. "That is us, with Gerard's father-in-law," he said, pointing at a picture of a young couple, sitting on a table, with an older man in a chef's apron standing beside them. "That was taken just before the war."

"*Before* the war?" I asked in disbelief.

"Yes, we really are that ancient," he joked, smiling at his elderly wife.

"I'm sorry to bother you, sir, but could you look at this photograph and tell me if anyone looks familiar?" I asked, showing him the picture that was most important to us.

"Well, that's Modigliani, the great painter, but I'm afraid I don't know the others."

"Not even the little girl?" Ana and Juliette said at the same time.

"Sorry, but…" he said, stopping short. "Wait a second," he said, then took the photograph over to show it to his wife.

"That's crazy Sylvia," the wrinkled lady said.

"Crazy Sylvia?" I asked anxiously as we all hurried over to her table.

"Yes. I ought to know. I worked in her fragrance house back in the seventies. Don't you remember?" she asked her husband.

"Ah, yes, Sylvia Chantly. Her perfumery is in Grasse, one of the oldest in the area. You can get there in less than an hour by car, and anyone can show you where it is. I haven't heard a word about Sylvia in decades, not that she was very social back in the day. She liked no one."

We thanked the couple and Monsieur Gerard, hopped in our rental car, and floored it to Grasse, a small town just north of Cannes. It made sense that a perfumery would be there, because Grasse was considered the scented luxuries capital of the world. Its inland location and its high altitude made for a microclimate that encouraged flower growth.

We drove for half an hour down winding roads that carried us upward. Several times, we stopped to inquire about the location of Chantly Perfumery. After getting lost twice, we finally found the place.

Like the other perfumeries we saw on the way, the place was on a huge plot of land. The distillery factory was a huge building in the back, and the front part had been made into a museum. We parked the car and went in with a fresh busload of tourists.

We agreed that we should visit the museum to learn as much as we could, so I stopped by the ticket booth to pay for our admission.

"A guided tour will start in ten minutes," the girl behind the counter said.

The guide, a young man named Patrick, started the tour in a big hall. "This was the site of the original distillery," he said, "before it moved to the other building in the back. This perfumery was founded in 1897, by Monsieur Henry Chantly. In the beginning, it employed only thirty people in the factory and on the farmland a few kilometers away. Back then, they harvested around fifteen tons a year of jasmine, roses, violets, gardenias, and other flowers," Patrick said, pointing at several old photographs on the wall as we walked by.

All four of us stared at each photo. The first showed a man in his forties, cutting a red ribbon in front of the perfumery. In another, he was standing in a vast field off roses, joined by several smiling faces. There were three or more other photos of him and others in different parts of the distillery. The last photos had been taken more recently, because the signs of age in Monsieur Henry were evident.

The guide then went into more detail about the harvesting process, the distillation, the production of single-floral fragrances, and the glassware in which the scents were stored. Designer crystal, gold-plated, and intricately carved bottles were on display in several places throughout the museum.

"Monsieur Henry died in 1914, at the age of 58, while on a cruise with his pregnant wife and a couple of their friends. She was twenty-five years her junior. It is said that he fell from the boat late at night and drowned in the sea," Patrick said, wearing a sad face.

"Did he have too much to drink?" one of the tourists asked.

"Well, Monsieur Henry and his wife, Madam Bernadette, loved to party and were known for a rather wild social life."

"Smart answer," the tourist replied, with a German accent in his voice.

"Madam Bernadette took over the business in 1914, but it was not a successful venture for her. She had no experience in the industry and was too much of a socialite. She was also very extravagant in her spending. She organized grand parties and gatherings. Most agreed that it was a blessing when Bernadette resigned in 1940, and her only daughter, Madam Sylvia, took over at the age of 26," the tour guide said as he led us toward the offices.

The moment he said Sylvia's name, we all looked at each other and smiled like kids with fresh candy.

"Madam Bernadette died a few years later, after she resigned," Patrick said, looking at the German. "As for Madam Sylvia, she was very different from her mother. She dedicated her life to her work and isolated herself from the media and, to an exaggerated extent, from most people in general. She was such a recluse that many claimed she was only seen at work from eight in the morning till six in the evening. During her years of service here, there were two expansions to the facility. The perfumery began selling in other markets, like detergents, shampoos, deodorants, creams, and cosmetics. Our exports increased from only ten countries to over sixty, and production was ten times as demanding as before. Madam Sylvia was the start of the golden era. She resigned 1985 and died eight years later, in 1993. She had one daughter, Madam Simone, by her first husband, whom she divorced after several years. Madam Simone took over when her mother passed, and she is in charge of Chantly Perfumery as we speak," the young man concluded as he pointed to the photo of the present owner.

I found it a bit odd that the museum had no photos of Madam Bernadette or Madam Sylvia, yet they did have one of Madam Simone, so I quickly went to young man and asked him about that.

"As I said, those two were not fond of photographs," he said, sounding a bit unsure and unconvincing.

"Is it possible to meet Madam Simone?" I asked. "I have some important business to discuss with her."

"I'm not sure that is feasible, sir. It is Saturday, and she is probably at home."

"Can we visit her there?" Ana asked, laying on the charm.

"Well, if you are fit, you could walk. The road to get there is too steep and narrow for most cars. I am from Nice, and the first time I drove to her place, I broke my front windows," Patrick kindly warned.

"We can walk," I said, confident that the professor's cane could carry me anywhere.

"Just go to the end of Rue de l'Ancien Palais De Justice, and take a right, then follow the road to the end. Her house is on the right. You can't miss it. It's huge, maybe the biggest in all Grasse," he said.

"Thank you, Patrick," I said, then shook his hand.

We decided that while Ana, Juliette, and I visited the woman, Patrice would take the car and pay a visit to one of the flower farms a few kilometers south. "Hopefully, a couple with their teenage daughter won't alarm her too much," I jested.

I had to stop twice during the walk, because my knee began to hurt a bit. After I rested a minute, with the help of my cane from one side and Ana on the other, I championed my way up. Juliette arrived at the placard about five minutes before us and shouted over her shoulder, "We made it! Chateau De Chantly."

It looked like a mansion or a castle, with at least fifteen hectares of land, with large meadows surrounding it. The chateau was made of gray stone, with floor-to-ceiling windows and ten huge columns in the front. From where we were standing, I could count at least twenty rooms, and the whole place was remarkable.

The white gates were open already, as if to welcome us in. We walked slowly, all three of us close together, passing rows of red and white roses that lined the path. The chateau appeared bigger with every step we took.

There were some cars near the entrance, including a black Rolls-Royce, a red Porsche, and a black Jeep. They were all parked around a big fountain that was carved in the shape of a tree, spurting water in all directions.

We were only halfway to the door when a voice called out to us from a small storage room on the right. A woman in a floppy, handwoven garden hat approached, carrying a pruner in her hand.

"I bet it's her," Juliette whispered in my ear.

"It is," I said.

She had aged a bit since the photograph at the museum was taken, but she was still very attractive. Her long, auburn hair reached her shoulders, and her eyes were big and blue and stood out against her olive-colored skin in lovely contrast. "Hello! How may I help you?" Madam Simone asked.

"I am Sebastian, and this is my wife, Ana, and our daughter, Juliette. This might seem very strange, but I would like to ask a few things about your mother," I said, handing her the photograph we'd brought with us.

She examined the picture for a few minutes, then looked up at me. "What is this in regard to?" she asked. "And where did you get this photo?"

"I own an art gallery in Paris, and I am deeply involved with a project about the painter Modigliani. I know this is your mother in this photograph with him. It was taken in front of a restaurant in Nice, around 1917," I said. "We believe there might be a connection."

"Excuse my ignorance. I am sorry, but I know little about the arts. That is my mother though," she said, confused.

"Can you tell us anything about her, your parents, grandparents, anyth—" I started to plead, but she held a hand up to stop me.

"A connection, you say? I doubt it. You must be mistaken, because Mother hated art. We don't even have a single painting in our house, because she wouldn't allow it. I'm surprised this photograph exists, because she disliked them as well. She only kept one or two of her own childhood, and she stored those with her private belongings that are still in her room to this day." She pointed to the third window to the right, on the second floor. "Her room is still intact, just as she left it, as is my grandfather's."

"No photos or paintings? She didn't allow it? I don't understand," Juliette questioned.

"I don't even have a photograph of my grandmother anywhere. Mother never talked about her," Madam Simone replied.

"We were just at the museum, and we didn't see any photographs of your mother or grandmother there," I replied.

"My mother was homeschooled because she couldn't stand being around other students. Still, she lifted this business to where it is today, all on her own and in a terrible time of war and financial crisis. I assure you that art was not her thing. She even bought a local art magazine back in the late forties, just to shut it down."

"Wow. That is shocking," I said.

"I am sorry I can't be of help. Is there anything else you need to know?" she asked, eager to get back to her daily routine.

I felt disappointment creeping into every part of me, but I thanked the woman, and we all made our way out the huge white gates and down the hill.

As we walked back to town, I pondered all we'd been told. *Sylvia hated paintings and photos, even other students, thus homeschooled. She wanted to live in total isolation, not at all like her mother, who loved parties and socializing. Did she really buy a local art magazine just to shut it down? She never talked about her mother either. Did she hate her? Why? Was she ashamed? What for?*

Then, suddenly, it all dawned on me. "It was her mother!"

"What?" Juliette asked, looking at me as if I'd lost my mind.

"She was ashamed of something, something to do with art," I shouted, then turned around to head back to the chateau, ignoring the pain in my knee.

By the time I got to the gates again, with Ana and Juliette in tow, Madam Simone was busy cutting some roses.

"You… You said she had her own room, stored all her belongings there," I said, laboring for breath.

"Yes. There are dozens of rooms in the estate. I haven't entered her quarters in years. When she died, we donated her jewelry to several charities, according to her wishes, but everything else is untouched. Only the maid goes in there, to dust things off every now and then," Madam Simone said.

"Would you mind if I take a look?" I asked. "I believe we may find the answers we're looking for, and you may learn some things as well."

Madam Simone removed her big bonnet and walked us all inside. We climbed a marble staircase to get to the second floor. She called the maid to ask for the key, and we stepped into her mother's room.

Everything was covered in white sheets. In the first area, there were sofas, tables, and a piano hiding under the coverings. There were about ten mirrors hangings on the walls, but no other decorations.

"No paintings or photographs here," I muttered to myself.

The maid then opened another door, which led to the bedroom. It was about the size of my flat in Paris. The king-sized bed was also covered with white sheets, as was the small sofa that faced the window that offered a serene view of the gardens and flowers below. There were two dressing tables, two small chairs, and what seemed to be a round table. Again, mirror after mirror lined the walls.

"The dressing room is on the right," the maid said, pointing. "There are clothes in there and lots and lots of boxes."

I walked into the dressing room with the three women behind me. We saw racks upon racks of clothes, shoes, and garment bags and boxes, all stored neatly. "May I?" I asked.

With Madam Simone's permission, we began going through the dozens of boxes. The first few only contained files and paperwork, along with a few old baccarat crystal jars, some hats and dresses and rugs.

I pulled another box out and opened it, but before I could say a word, Juliette came running over to me.

"Dad, look!" she cried, holding out a magazine with a painting of a nude woman on the cover. "It's Madam

Bernadette, and there are dozens of copies of this edition in that box."

"I see," I said to Juliette as I pulled a rolled painting from the box I'd opened a moment before. I then carefully unfolded Modigliani's painting of Madam Bernadette.

No one said a word. We all just stared at the precious parcel we'd found. I felt tears filling my eyes, and I saw them also welling in the gorgeous eyes of the two greatest loves of my life. Madam Simone, stunned, teared up as well.

A short while later, I called Patrice to let him know our great news. I invited him to the chateau for dinner, on Madam Simone's insistence.

"Madam Simone, what you have here is worth tens of millions of dollars. I'm not sure what your plans are for the treasure, but I wanted to mention that," I said as we all sat at the beautiful oak table in her dining room, under an enormous, red crystal chandelier.

"My work at the perfumery, my family legacy, has already blessed me with millions. If that painting was yours, what would you do with it?" she asked.

"First, I would put my expertise to work to restore the painting to its best possible condition," I said. "That would take a year or more to finish. I hope that doesn't offend you, since it is a painting of your grandmother, but I would then display it in my gallery for a year. After that, I would lease it to museums everywhere, so art lovers all around the world could enjoy its beauty. Then, hmm... I suppose I—"

"Then," Juliette cut in, "we would sell it and use the money to open many schools in Africa, to eradicate illiteracy in all those villages."

I smiled at my daughter, and I couldn't have been prouder of her. She was a mirror image of her mother, and that was the greatest compliment I could give her.

"Schools in Africa?" Madam Simone inquired.

"Sebastian and I honeymooned in Kenya nearly twenty years ago," Ana said, holding Juliette's hand. "We were touched by the sad conditions we saw there, especially for the children and their young, widowed mothers, so we decided to help as much as possible. We've held several exhibitions throughout the years and donated the profits to the building of schools in that impoverished area, to give those children a chance for a better life. We've opened eight schools so far, and we hope to do much more."

"Interesting. My son would love to hear it. He works with the Médecins Sans Frontières and spends a lot of his time in Africa and other places. I have always supported his ethics, his yearning to help those in need, even though it takes him away from me for much of the time." She paused, then continued, "My mother chose to hide the painting. Perhaps it caused her some embarrassment during her childhood. I respect that, but it was my grandmother's choice to be drawn in such manner, and I respect that as well. I will agree to the terms you've mentioned, except that 10 percent will be cut from the final sale value, 5 percent for your gallery and 5 percent for me. I have a project in my mind for the locals, and I'd prefer not to use the money earned at the perfumery. With the remainder, your beautiful Ana and Juliette, along with my son, will open schools for those in need, all over the world."

Speechless, we all just stared at her, then looked at one another.

"Well? Shall we drink to that?" the woman said, raising her glass.

I looked at all the smiling faces around the table. "Absolutely! I will drink a whole bottle to that!" I said.

Epilogue

After nearly everyone left the auction house, I stood alone, looking at the 170,000,000 pounds-valued painting of Madam Bernadette, by the great Modigliani. Before I sold it, over 5,000,000 people had seen it all over the world.

For three years, that painting hung on museum walls in Paris, New York, London, Madrid, Chicago, Tokyo, Vienna, Amsterdam, Rome, Buenos Aires, Moscow and other cities. Now, millions of others would be privileged to gaze at it too, for I knew its new owner, Mr. Arnold would surely share the beauty like I had. His love for art had no boundaries, and it was a passion we shared.

At the same time, the sale meant hundreds of thousands of people who'd been deprived of a proper education would have a chance for a brighter future. They would become doctors and engineers, teachers and musicians, maybe even artists themselves.

I kissed the painting goodbye and went out to join my daughter, who was waiting anxiously under her umbrella, happily talking to her mother on phone. Our flight would carry us back home in a few hours, and the two of them were already preparing a celebration at the gallery later that night. I promised to play my guitar for them till the early hours of dawn as long as my band included Idris, Antoine, Emilie, and they did all the singing.

The End

About the Author

Ahmad Ardalan is a two-time cancer survivor. He was born in Baghdad in 1979. At the age of two, he moved with his parents to Vienna, Austria, where he spent most of his childhood and underwent his primary studies. After his father's diplomatic mission finished at the end of 1989, he returned to Iraq, where he continued his studies and graduated from the University of Dentistry. As a result of the unstable political, military, social, and economic conditions in his home country, Ahmad decided to leave Iraq and move to the UAE. After facing difficulties to pursue his career in dentistry, he opted to pursue employment in the business world. Since then, Ardalan has held several senior roles within the pharmaceutical and FMCG industries, throughout much of the Middle East. His early childhood in a mixed cultural environment, as well as his world travels, increased his passion for learning about cultures of the world and inspired him to pen The Clout of Gen, his first novel. After eleven years of being away, Ahmad returned to Baghdad in January 2013 on a visit that was full of mixed emotions. Inspired by his trip to Iraq, he wrote his second novel, The Gardener of Baghdad. He did not stop there, as "Matt" his latest Short Story Thriller Series became available beginning 2015. The Gardener of Baghdad, opened readers' eyes to a different picture of the city they had heard of. With hope and love as his message, Ardalan released Baghdad: The Final Gathering, and followed it by The Boy of the Mosque. A recent visit to Paris, and its lovely museums, and galleries inspired him to write his latest novel, The Art Collector of Le Marais.

Other Publications by Ahmad Ardalan:

The Gardener of Baghdad

"Two people, one city, different times; connected by a memoir. Can love exist in a city destined for decades of misery?"

Adnan leads a weary existence as a bookshop owner in modern-day, war-torn Baghdad, where bombings, corruption and assault are everyday occurrences and the struggle to survive has suffocated the joy out of life for most. But when he begins to clean out his bookshop of forty years to leave his city in search of somewhere safer, he comes across the story of Ali, the Gardener of Baghdad, Adnan rediscovers through a memoir handwritten by the gardener decades ago that beauty, love and hope can still exist, even in the darkest corners of the world.

The Boy of the Mosque

In the Year 1258, Baghdad, the capital of the great Abbasid Caliphate, fell to the Moguls. Within hours, the city of enlightenment was swallowed up by darkness, another society becoming a victim of hatred and greed. The mighty Tigris flowed with blue and red, the blood of its people and the ink from the age-old scrolls of knowledge, all heartlessly washed away.

In spite of the turmoil and chaos, twelve families managed to flee. Far away they wandered, leaving behind their beautiful homeland that had been reduced to death and rubble. Together, that remnant from Baghdad established a new community, one that lived in peace and harmony for centuries.

Centuries later, in 2017, mercenaries and militias took over that charming village, threatening to destroy the happy existence the people had worked so hard to rebuild. What will be the fate of those innocent people and their heritage? That hangs in the balance as all must rely on one man, The Boy of the Mosque...

Baghdad: The Final Gathering

"Wars, an embargo, and forbidden love in this once peaceful city..."

With the drums of war just weeks away, Omar invites all those closest to his heart for lunch at his lavish villa overlooking the Tigris River of Baghdad. He can't help but smile at the faces that have graced his eventful life that spans from an interesting childhood, the two Gulf Wars, and the inhumane embargo that crippled the nation. Loved ones come together, probably for the last time, in the city their ancestors called Baghdad or Baghdadu, *"God's Gift."*
Memories upon memories linger in Omar's head. He has survived times of struggle, holding on to hope and love along the way. As he reflects on his journey, as a man destined to live a hard life in tumultuous times, he ponders a clouded future, on the brink of unknown change.

The Clout of Gen

"What if major events in modern history were planned decades ago?"

Newspaper reporter John Teddy's miserable life is turned upside down when he uncovers a voice from the past—a voice that suspiciously knows far too much about the would-be future. John's natural curiosity to understand the hidden message takes him to places he never imagined seeing, and ongoing conspiracies he never thought existed. The more John gets involved, the more he is led towards mysteries that are beyond his understanding. The circle of people involved grows bigger stretching from west to east; each step forward is like a step backward.

Matt Vol I

"They murdered my wife two years ago...
Tonight, you die.
I am Matt, your nightmare!"

On a quiet night like any other, Matt, a successful entrepreneur, returns home to his gorgeous villa, only to find his wife brutally murdered. A soft verdict against the culprits, a gang of violent teenagers, spins Matt's relatively calm and collected demeanor into something far more sinister. In a manic rage, he seeks vengeance for what has been stolen from him, and he lashes out against the weak system. Sleepless, lonely, tormented nights torture him, filling his head and his heart with frustration, hate, and anger, unleashing an entirely different side of the man--a monster even he did not know existed within him. From Berlin to Rome to Paris, the great cities of the world suffer in the wake of his wrath, as brutal, barbaric killings seem to be the only temporary antidote for his fuming, blood-boiling rage. His victims, so easily deprived of life, seem to be the only cure, the only way to soothe his yearning for revenge, or are they?

Matt Vol II: Chaos in Dubai

"They tried hard to stop me. But, even I can't stop myself"

In the bustling city of Dubai, the new theater for his manic actions, Matt faces his worst enemy: a deep inner struggle for identity. Part of him craves the recognition a media frenzy and a new infamous nickname grant him, for he feels his murders are works of art that demand attention, but a love interest reawakens another part of him, reigniting an innocence he once carried within. Can love overcome hate in a city that prides itself on being a luxurious safe haven? As the end nears, which version of Matt will he be?

Matt Vol III: Hunterman

"Am I being hunted?
Think again. I am Matt, I am the hunter.."

The dark trilogy reaches its ultimatum, as Manic Matt approaches The Feds to takedown Hunterman. Would they work with a serial killer for a better cause? Could The Feds trust a man, half the world is chasing? A psychopath of many faces?